# Acknowledgements

I want to take a moment to express my sincere gratitude to the individuals who took time out of their busy schedules to read, offer feedback, and encourage the publication of this book.  These people have been involved in the athletic community as a parent, coach, teacher, and/or mentor. Your feedback and confidence in the message of this book truly means a lot. Thank you all!

Virginia Gabel

Don Sigmund

Chris & Angela Seymour

Ted

# Dedication

This book is dedicated to God.

I pray that this book serves you, glorifies you,

and leads people to you.


*Bless everyone reading this book.*


My prayer is that you use these words to help people find healing, discover their purpose...and embrace your truth.

# Endorsement

Playing your sport is what you do, not who you are.

Dee Shaffer's book, "1000%" can help you get off the emotional roller coaster that high level sports can be and restore the joy of competition.

**Walt Day**
*Director of Athletes In Action, Pro Sports Ministry for New England.*
*Chaplain for New England Patriots 1993-2006*
*Baseball Chapel Leader of Boston Red Sox 1995-2008.*

# Table of Contents

# Chapter 1

# YOU

I f you are an athlete...

This book is written especially for you.

It is intended to reach deep inside and help you see yourself from the inside out rather than the outside in. From the stunning depths of your soul rather than the prowess of your physical talent. This book will recognize the rare environment you find yourself in and will help you comprehend perhaps why you are here.

Prepare yourself to be deeply challenged, perhaps even convicted in places. But most of all be prepared to embrace that you have been chosen, selected, and hand-picked by the Lord to be *exactly* where you are at this very point in time. This book will offer truth. Truth that does not necessarily come from the athletic community, your coach, society, your parents, or even yourself. It will offer truth that comes from God and will help you understand how that truth manifests in your life and how it can radically change everything. Buckle up.

Hear this truth.

You are truly extraordinary, and you need to know that God has an *incredible* purpose for your life.

It may not feel that way after watching your performance statistics plummet at times, or feeling the intense desire to quit the team, or to fight off tormenting anxiety every second of your life. But please allow me to walk through all of this and help you see why you have been chosen to walk this path, with both all of its rewards and all of its suffering.

Everyone is on their own journey with their own particular stressors in life. An athlete is as well, but incredibly, the athlete has additional pressures that come from every imaginable angle and source. These extra pressures can and do cause significant distress. It can be a heavy burden for many, and sadly it can have adverse effects on a person's mental health as well as their athletic performance. This only exacerbates and already spiraling cycle.

I will briefly share my personal experience only to offer some credibility to the knowledge and awareness of athletic pressure. I will then walk with you as we dissect the types of stress felt by the athlete, and ways in which this stress can be put into better perspective and hopefully lighten its intensity. At the end of this book, you will hopefully begin to recognize the foundation of your incredible purpose and will begin to see how God has woven his strength, his grace, and his authority into you so that you can fulfill that purpose.

To begin, I began life in a very difficult place, growing up in an unhealthy and challenging environment. I was stunted intellectually and I did not do well academically for a number of reasons. Without getting into detail, my life was overwhelming and I was extremely lost in its dark grip.

I was very athletic, however. Athletic achievement came naturally to me as I discovered I could throw a baseball like a cannon and catch a football better than all the boys in my town. I played on the boys' sports teams and even chased a few into centerfield a few times to make sure they didn't disrespect me...again.

I found myself achieving a lot of success with sports and it allowed me to receive positive attention from my accomplishments. In all honesty, sports were a saving grace for me in many ways, because without them, I am not sure where my life would have led me.

My best two sports happened to be volleyball and basketball. I was offered a scholarship to play NCAA Division II basketball while in high school, and during my senior year, I signed a letter of intent to play. Just a few weeks into my season, I found myself in the hospital for the next three months and missed almost all of my final year of high school basketball due to a medical emergency with one of my lungs. All attempts to treat my condition failed so my lung had to be surgically stitched to my chest wall and I was eventually able to be released from the hospital. Obviously, as a result of this devastation, I missed nearly all of the basketball season during my senior year of high school. It was distressing, as basketball was my scholarship-my ticket to a better life, higher education, and a chance to finally make it out of the traps of my childhood.

Fortunately, I was able to heal sufficiently to make it to the NCAA DII basketball camp the following summer and I learned that my scholarship was not retracted. I went on to play. While I was at the university, I was "talked into" running the half mile for the track team, so, I did that as well. When my sophomore year rolled around, I discovered my father was terminally ill. I transferred to a different university closer to him and played volleyball and basketball my junior and senior years.

Clearly, my life had its complexities and challenges just like other people who don't play sports, but it also had the added intense pressure of playing competitively at the NCAA level. It didn't occur to me that three sports in college was a bit much, so I willingly accepted all the opportunities I had available to me.

I share all of that *only* to provide a foundation from a perspective of having experienced high intensity stress in an athletic environment. I know about all the anxiety, and repeated thoughts of failure, and feelings of defeat that an athlete has to battle day in and day out. You love the sport but it is not always fun and it is never easy. Sometimes (perhaps all the time) you feel like you actually hate it because the demands and pressures are so great.

It can get deeper than that, and it does. Often, like me, an athlete will be so consumed with their sport and all that goes into it, that being an athlete becomes their identity. It happened to me as a young girl as I realized that sports were the only positive in my life. I clung to athletics and my actual name literally became synonymous with basketball, volleyball, track, and softball. All were inextricably linked to me and therefore my athletic ability naturally became my identity.

As we walk through your life as an athlete, we will unpack all the positives and negatives that combine together and fiercely push you to the brink of exhilaration and also the brink of overwhelming defeat. A cycle that takes its toll physically, mentally, spiritually, and emotionally.

We will also look deeply into your situation from a spiritual perspective to help you comprehend this incredible purpose you are being shaped for. We will attempt to look at sports through the eyes of God and how he wants us to see and experience them in our lives. This will be the most important message of this book, and I have confidence that it will encourage and uplift you as you are able to recognize that God is not the pressure you feel or the anxiety that courses through your veins. No. He is the one holding you up and keeping your head above water until you are finally able to see him.

*"Even to your old age and gray hairs I am he, I am he who will sustain you. I have made you and I will carry you"* Isaiah 46:4

*"For I am the Lord your God who takes hold of your right hand and says to you, do not fear; I will help you"* Isaiah 41:13

*"He gives strength to the weary. and increases the power of the weak"* Isaiah 40:29

Now, let's get into some substance that I pray will help you identify your incredible purpose more clearly and help offer some healing perspectives that you can have complete confidence in.  Let's seek out the only truth that can remove the overwhelming pressure you carry and the dreadful anxiety that you host.

But first let's establish a few points of agreement as we go through this.

It is important that you read each scripture that is presented in the book.  Scriptures are essential and are literally what provides the power of any message delivered.  Everything else is just words. You are seeking life-changing perspectives, right?  Yes? Then I encourage you to read the scriptures, as they provide the foundation for the message in this book and are the only truths that can reach you and change your life.

*"For the word of God is alive and active. Sharper than any double-edged sword, it penetrates even to dividing soul and spirit, joints and marrow; it judges the thoughts and attitudes of the heart."* Hebrews 4:12

*"In the beginning was the Word, and the Word was with God, and the Word was God."* John 1

When you read scripture, you can see it is actually *alive*, has the ability to *penetrate* all, and is literally *God*. Even if you can't understand this right now, it is important for you to have this knowledge. Perhaps one day you will fully comprehend how incredibly powerful this truth is.

Finally, we want to invite the Lord directly into this message for you individually. Let's pray in agreement and ask Him to use these words to reach you, heal you, encourage you, and put you on the path He has for you. God is not oppressive or dominating. He respects your choices whether you make decisions with or without Him. I encourage you to invite Him into your life to help you. He is knocking at the door of your heart just waiting for you to open it.

*"Behold, I stand at the door and knock. If anyone hears My voice and opens the door, I will come in to him and dine with him, and he with Me." Revelation 3:20*

*"For where two or three gather in my name, there am I with them." Matthew 18:20*

Lord,

Thank you for leading me and guiding me to your truth and to your Word. I am but a person who is lost without you and I am humbly seeking your help, guidance, love, and direction. I have been provided with gifts and talents and I want to use them to serve You. I need to know you are with me as my life is filled with blessings, yet it is enormously challenging and difficult. I am seeking wisdom from You and the knowledge of Your saving grace as I move forward in life on this day. I know I am not perfect and that you are. Jesus Christ died for my imperfections and I humbly accept this gift and believe in Him to save me. I pray this in His name. Amen.

*"For God so loved the world, that he gave his only begotten Son, that whosoever believeth in him should not perish, but have everlasting life. For God sent not his Son into the world to condemn the world; but that the world through him might be saved." John 3:16-17*

# Chapter 2

# FOUNDATION

Sports are fun!  Not only are they fun, but they teach us countless lessons and they help us build and develop internal strength, self-discipline, and the ability to work with a team. For some, sports offer an avenue to express natural talents and find success.  Combining dedication and talent toward something can offer great rewards and often does.  An athlete understands this because there is no success without first, a natural talent and second, applying the talent through training regimes.

Being an athlete often brings a significant amount of positive attention and for some it can offer frequent high-level praise.  At some level, this can be healthy as it will often influence a person to head down a positive, constructive path in life and open doors for them to express their God-given talents and gifts.  That is precisely what we are to do in this life-utilize the talents and gifts that we have been given.  But there is much more to this than meets the eye.  It goes far deeper than just utilizing gifts and talents, however, that part will be revealed later in this book.

For now, I will talk about how this very scenario can and often does, incubate a deeply agonizing, unwanted vine that often finds itself choking out these blessings.  It is this very weed that grows its roots right alongside these God-given gifts and entwines itself around and through the heart and mind of many, many athletes.

Let's consider some real scenarios.

Jordan was a Division I volleyball player. She had incredible natural talent as an athlete and was internally driven to excel in sports from the minute she began participating as an 8-year-old girl on "Play Day" in elementary school. She was tall and strong as a child and very athletically gifted. Naturally, she gravitated to sports and did what most people would do, and developed an intense interest in athletics.

As is quite normal in elementary school, girls mature faster than boys, so because of this, Jordan dominated a lot of the boys on the playground and was always one of the first kids chosen in competitive games. So, you can see how her success was developed by her natural talent and reinforced by frequent positive attention as it related to her athletics.

As years progressed, Jordan tried out for every sport possible in Middle School and High School. She was a Varsity athlete every year in three sports, and on top of that, she played on a competitive volleyball team as well as a competitive softball team. She achieved significant athletic accomplishments in multiple sports and earned All-Conference and All-State awards.

By all appearances, Jordan was finding success and was walking gracefully into numerous gold medal opportunities, and it appeared to come easy for her. The community she grew up in, her friends, peers, sports reporters, and coaches saw these outcomes and openly and secretly evaluated, criticized, judged, or glorified her.

Jordan was literally swimming in a sea of external judgment from a very young age, and she was powerfully influenced and shaped by the multitude of voices in her athletic world. Combine this dynamic with her deeply driven personality, she eventually found herself facing her greatest competitor of all time. Fear.

Jordan's internal drive was fueled and intensified by the external voices and she pushed herself to continue to excel in whatever sport she was engaged in. If she didn't excel, she read discouraging words in the sports articles, felt awkward tension with her teammates, and was constantly wondering what her coach was thinking. This reality found a place deep within and accompanied her off the volleyball court and followed her to bed every night. It never departed from her, even though the game was long over.

Conversely, Jordan would hear the cheers and accolades about her abilities after a great athletic performance, and these encouraging external judgements would powerfully influence her as well. She valued and enjoyed hearing positive comments and reading about her "stellar" performance in the newspaper and on social media the next day. These scenarios reinforced her as a person and she consciously and subconsciously pursued performance at a level to maintain this kind of praise.

In the short 10 years, from age 8-18, two deeply rooted realities became entwined with each other and both were constantly fighting for dominion over the other. One was Jordan's natural God-given talent and who God created her to be, and the other was the fear she developed as a result of the judgments she faced *because of* her talent. This dynamic was subconsciously developing and growing inside her with each passing year, and Jordan was constantly strategizing how to overcome the increasing heaviness these forces had on her life.

By the time Jordan graduated high school, these dynamics had grown with her and were so deeply entwined, that they had attached themselves to her identity.  At this point, she was unable to recognize that she had assumed these external and internal gifts and judgments as her identity.  To the world she was Jordan the athlete.  But inside she was being eaten alive by fear and its favorite manifestation. Anxiety.

Few, if anyone, knew about the ravaging effects that fear had on her.  In fact, it would be safe to say that almost no one considered that she experienced any fear at all, let alone be consumed by it.  But she was up against fierce, invisible opposition with no play book, no coach, and no meaningful understanding of it.  Any athlete will tell you that this is an unfair fight and that it is impossible to be victorious over a formidable opponent that you know nothing about.

As the forces would have it, Jordan secured a nice athletic scholarship to play volleyball at a NCAA Division I University.  Celebrations were in order, social media lit up like it was ESPN Sports Center, and her athleticism took front and center stage in the life of everyone around her.

Jordan was elated, humbled, thrilled, proud....and terrified.

But again, no one really knew this because she kept it to herself and being the athlete that she was, it was not acceptable to show fear to anyone.  Fear represented weakness and a target for others to exploit. It would offer up doubt in the minds of her coaches. So, she buried it.

As Jordan moved states away from her hometown of 18 years to attend university and play volleyball, she realized before classes even started that she was basically owned by her sport.  No longer could she run to Taco Bell at 5:30, or plan to go out with friends.

Perhaps some of these opportunities were there, but she was completely exhausted from the 4-hour practices 6 days a week, a weight training program 5 days a week, all wedged in the challenging pre-req's she was taking.

This was her new physical reality, which by all accounts was difficult. But I am going to demonstrate how these physical challenges paled in comparison to the emotional, mental, psychological, and spiritual anguish that ravaged her life – every moment of every day.

Going off to play volleyball at a higher level had its perks. The scholarship was very nice, the university was amazing, and it was a life event that allowed her independence from home and parents, and it gave her plenty of glory to be one of the less-than 2% of athletes to play at an NCAA Division I level. Who should be complaining, right?

Well, she wasn't. She was literally trying to live off the fumes of this image and keep silent about the jagged fear that was consuming her.

As Jordan did all she could to maintain her focus on her talents and accomplishments just to remind herself that she is worthy to be there, her phone would light up with countless notifications of social media commentary, judgments, and criticisms of literally everyone she knew, including herself. She saw selfies posted every 2 seconds of girls in their bikinis, athletes blasting a kill at the 10-foot line, and an unlimited supply of fake images of perfection.

The roots of Jordan's false identity were about to begin producing their fruit. She would soon discover that most of this fruit was going to be bitter, rotten, and toxic.

# Chapter 3

# GROUND & SOIL

I want you to shift your mind a little and think about agriculture. More specifically, think about wheat. For just a minute, let's review its basic lifecycle that was taught to us in 8th grade.

1. In order for a plant to develop, there must be a seed.

2. The seed needs to be planted in order to grow.

3. The roots of this plant must have fertile soil in which to draw proper nutrients for the plant to grow.

4. If these essential elements are present, then the plant can eventually produce their fruit (mature wheat head ready for harvest).

That is the basic life cycle of all living things. Agree?

If we were to take a grain of wheat and toss it onto the hard surface of the ground, what would it do? It would just sit there and exist in its grain-like state. It might get blown around by the wind, or rained on, or even get dried out by the scorching sun. But it would not produce one stalk of wheat.

However, if the soil was tilled or plowed, and the grain was tossed into the broken soil, it would be able to germinate, receive proper nutrients and moisture and would grow into a mature stalk of wheat.

The soil had to be broken in order for the grain to develop and produce its fruit.

*The soil had to be broken.*

The human experience is very similar to this analogy.

We all start out the same. We grow and develop and ultimately, we produce fruit. That fruit might be healthy or it might resemble a destructive weed that tries to obstruct and strangle everything healthy around it. But neither the good or the destructive can grow without something breaking in order for it to take root.

I think it is safe to say that not one person is perfect or grows up without pain or distress of some sort. Life is difficult and we are victims of our circumstances sometimes and we can also create some difficulties all on our own. That is just a fact and it applies to everyone.

But it is these difficult moments and these distressing times that cause us to "break" internally to some degree. It is like the plow that breaks up soil. A significant stressor can be hurtful and cause emotional pain or some level of heartbreak. Some people experience more heartbreak than others, but no one can walk through life without experiencing some degree of pain from a life event.

These moments, at face value, are normal and are experienced by all. Again, some have more wounds than others, but the concept remains the same.

Visualize that our minds, intellect, and thought processes serve as the ground surface, and our hearts serve as the soil beneath the surface that can allow a seed to take root and begin to grow. Consider that the seed represents judgments, comments, criticisms, love, care, and value. All the things that we experience that actually touch and reach our heart. It can be good, bad, healthy, or harmful. They are all seeds in this analogy.

Let's consider Jordan again. As she was growing up, just like anyone else, she experienced challenges, hard times, some trauma from perhaps divorce or difficult relationships. The same sort of complications that many people endure. Because these years were her formative years, all the good, bad, harsh, and loving experiences grew and developed with her. Along the way, she internalized all those external judgments and they wove themselves into her identity. They planted and rooted themselves in her heart and literally grew with her.

As with most athletes, the road to high performance and competitive opportunities begins in elementary school. When a child is eight or nine years old, we all know and understand that those years are considered our developmental years. A lot is being shaped and developed during this time and the hearts and minds of young children are literally being formed by their environment combined with their genetics.

It is difficult enough without having added pressures of sports, but for most of us reading this book, athletics played a major role in our developmental years and has woven its roots into our very own existence.

Let's consider James.

James lived with his family in the suburbs.  He was extraordinarily gifted at football.  He was tall, agile, and had a fantastic arm with precise aim.  He found himself excelling at the quarterback position beginning in elementary school when his parents signed him up for one of the many traveling football teams that were available outside the organized school district he attended.

He learned quickly, that being the quarterback of the football team demanded an extraordinary ability to handle harsh criticism by both his teammates as well as their families and all the fans in the stands.  Just being in that one position put him in a spotlight and the heaviness of the team's success was felt by James-week in and week out.  Clearly, the success of the team was not 100% on him, but perception heavily leaned that way and he felt each bit of negative energy that glared from countless eyes from age 8 all the way through high school.

James went on to play NCAA football and experienced moderate success, but he took with him the deeply held insecurity that was unwittingly created by years and years of glorified commentary and vicious disparagements that always seemed to find more space in his heart to exist.

As he grew from 4th grade in this environment, the comments entered his mind as he heard and read all the praise and all the criticism.  Those things began to take root in his heart, and when they did that, they were then able to grow.  As you recall, the heart is the fertile soil from what the mind receives.

As with Jordan, James continued to have success and of course performances that were less than impressive throughout high school and college.  As an athlete at the NCAA level, he was blasted with nothing but judgments and comments about his performance at every turn.  Social media became a deeply held addiction as he was incessantly drawn to the never-ending commentary about his athletic performance.

James was not about to intentionally show the world how it all affected him, so he naturally internalized it and found himself sliding deeper and deeper into alcohol, indiscriminate sex, wild parties, and anything at an extreme level that might bring him some momentary pleasure or happiness. He was desperate to counter the deep fear and insecurity he felt from the years of countless external voices creating his identity.

# Chapter 4

# DECEITFUL WEEDS

**M**ost of us are not experts in agriculture, so because of that, we cannot always recognize an authentic plant from a weed. Sometimes it is obvious, but not always. As we continue to examine the life of wheat, it is likely that many of us are unaware that there is a sinister counterpart that literally grows side by side with the healthy stalk of wheat.

This counterpart resembles, grows with, and is nearly indistinguishable from the wheat. In fact, it is so indistinguishable that it cannot be extracted and separated until the harvest. The extraction and separation processes are very harsh and frankly brutal, yet highly necessary in order for the authentic stalk of wheat to fulfill its intended purpose.

The heart of the athlete, again, is the fertile soil in which seeds are planted, and as we know, it takes a significant amount of time for seeds to develop into their mature states of existence. Whether we realize this or not, God has given each one of us very specific and unique talents, gifts, and callings. He has placed enormous value upon our individual lives and has implanted within each one of us, a very specific measure of faith. That faith is perhaps microscopic and beyond our awareness or comprehension, however, it exists deep within every living soul on this planet.

*"For I say, through the grace given to me, to everyone who is among you, not to think of himself more highly than he ought to think, but to think soberly, as God has dealt to each one a measure of faith"*
*Romans 12:3 NKJV*

This measure of faith, implanted by God, is within each of us. It is that living "grain of wheat" waiting for the soil to be broken so that it can drop in, receive nutrients, and begin to grow. But as we all understand, authentic seeds are planted intentionally and by choice. Weeds are not. They are wild and exist alongside healthy plants and we are constantly battling them and taking steps to eliminate them. This is a "law of nature" that most of us recognize, see, practice, and understand. It is a physical process and it makes sense to us naturally.

Take this natural analogy and apply it spiritually.

God has provided you with a seed of faith, but with that comes other seeds of doubt, fear, and many other harmful opposing forces. This concept is true in the natural, and it is also true in the spiritual. We have seemed to grasp it in the natural because we make every effort to nurture and care for the authentic seed and eliminate the weeds. If we don't understand this process spiritually, we unknowingly nurture and care for the weeds, which allows them to grow, strengthen, and produce their toxic fruit. If this process goes on uninterrupted, it will eventually strangle, overpower, and steal all the nutrients intended for the healthy seed.

The spiritual outcome of this means that the individual will be overcome with a spirit of fear, torment, anger, bitterness, or entitlement and endure its toxic manifestations of anxiety, depression, hopelessness, or worse. A weed cannot produce anything positive, so when it is unwittingly nurtured, its "fruit" will naturally take root and grow in the soil in which it is planted.

Athletes are people, so just like everyone else, they provide this same field, ground, and soil.  However, with an athlete, their field can be vast, and the seeds (judgements and experiences) that blow their way are numerous, relentless, and are not always recognizable as harmful. In fact, the judgements are often positive and glorifying.  They motivate the athlete and help propel them to continue their efforts to perform in ways to maintain this level of praise and admiration.

Athlete or not, this desire is present in all of us.  No one wants to pursue a path that invites constant negativity, degradation, and disapproval.  That isn't natural.  So clearly, the athlete is performing and expressing their natural talent, and the external approval and accolades reinforce their behavior.  The athletic performance and the approval of others become planted and begin to grow together.  They become inextricably linked at the incubation stage of development.  When this happens, I would venture a guess that it is this moment where their identity is formed.

A false identity.

This false identity is nearly impossible to recognize until its fruit begins to manifest its overwhelming toxicity, and forces the athlete to make significant changes.  Good, bad, or ugly.  Often, this very point of pressure, anxiety, and fear causes an internal break within the spirit of the athlete.  A moment that feels awful, horrible, and hopeless.  The athlete is likely consumed with jagged unease, ripping thoughts of failure, and paralyzing thoughts of ruin.  All of which has grown so prolifically inside them that they believe these messages and are seemingly at the mercy of this perceived "truth".

It is also just as likely that this reality is hidden from almost everyone around them because the athlete is keenly aware of and has learned to behave in ways that please others.  No way can or will the athlete show signs of weakness, a fracture of spirit, or a hint of insecurity.  So, they are held captive in their dark torment and continue to rely on these prolific weeds to help them overcome the toxicity that is destroying them.  Yet they are completely unaware that they are nurturing a full-grown enemy that exists inside them.

What is wrong with positive attention?

Nothing necessarily.  However, it is important to distinguish the positive attention and what it is attached to.  Is the positive attention attached to the athlete doing selfless things for others, God, being respectful of people, or honoring their parents, siblings, or others? Likely not.

The positive attention is most likely directed at their athletic performance.

This is still not a catastrophic reality.  However, it can, and often does, assign itself to performance and behavior targeted at pleasing the source of the positive attention. Athletic performance becomes enmeshed with the praise and admiration of those who pay attention to the athlete's statistics, contribution to the win, or where they rank amongst their counterparts in the league, division, or nation.  Athletic performance can literally become an obsession in order to garner more and more of this kind of approval and esteem.

When an athlete absorbs repeated avenues of glory and sometimes reverence, it produces an inherent awareness and belief that their athletic performance BECOMES their personal value.

I will argue that this is the worst possible scenario for any athlete.

If praise and adoration of good performance become so entangled in a person's psyche - to the point that it starts to define their value as a person (many athletes will understand this clearly), the battle has been won.

Why is this the worst possible scenario for an athlete?

Think about it.  If a person's value as a human being, is literally so deeply intertwined with their athletic performance, can you imagine the catastrophic consequences of having a bad game, a slump, or falling short of achieving the pre-season projections?

Frankly, the consequences are horrific.

I will share *one* outcome that perhaps leads some athletes to develop a full-blown mentality of superiority and perhaps, narcissism.  This mindset can turn a person into a deeply troubled individual that has advanced the need for praise into a controlling, self-absorbed demand.  This person will go to any length to recreate this need.  They will even get to the point of lying, bullying, rejecting, or abusing others in an effort to obtain the praise and reverence they so desperately crave and frankly need.

These individuals will intentionally surround themselves with others who are obsessed with their athletic prowess and accomplishments, or those who lack strength and insight, and allow themselves to be used to prop up, glorify, and cave to the worship demands of the athlete.  Both groups of people are magnets for these athletes because sadly, their value as a person has developed a dependency upon the admiration and approval of others.

It is my personal opinion that this continued state of being is very much the ultimate defeat.

Unfortunately, I believe that these people are so blind to their circumstance, that they do not and likely cannot recognize the horrific situation they are in.  They cannot see that they have become trapped in a squirrel cage that takes them nowhere, but keeps them perpetually imprisoned in their agonizing world of performance.  These people become their own god and generally cannot see beyond themselves.

It is the worst possible scenario, because if a person is blind to this reality, they will likely not seek help to draw them out of that downward spiral.  They will continue to control their environment in every way imaginable in order to demand the glory that they need.  Remember, their value as a person is most likely so deeply entangled with performance and praise, that it has developed into a life-or-death need.

Referring back to the agriculture cycle, these athletes are entirely unaware that they are feeding, watering, and nurturing a field of thorns, weeds, and barbs.  There is no "W" at the end of this game, and their performance, if not identified and corrected, will be harshly separated and subsequently burned up because it is not authentic mature wheat.  It is the weed *that resembles the wheat* at the time of harvest.

*"For men will be lovers of themselves, lovers of money, boasters, proud, blasphemers, disobedient to parents, unthankful, unholy, unloving, unforgiving, slanderers, without self-control, brutal, despisers of good, traitors, headstrong, haughty, lovers of pleasure rather than lovers of God, having a form of godliness but denying its power. And from such people turn away!" 2 Timothy 3:2-9 NKJV*

# Chapter 5

# Broken

The athlete just described, is likely not reading this book (or any similar resource). Instead, they are perhaps continuing to bask in the manufactured glory surrounding them which has created a blinding, false sense of stability, and an environment in which they can't recognize their own brokenness. Clearly, as for anyone, if there is not an awareness of brokenness, then there will not be an effort to find healing. That principle applies to everyone who has a pulse.

There is *another* large group of athletes who are experiencing brokenness as well. However, these individuals are deeply aware of their suffering, experience their wreckage with each breath, and are desperately doing all they can to just keep their head above water. These athletes are tormented with debilitating anxiety, profuse thoughts of defeat and hopelessness, and feel as though they are trapped in a world that they perceive as mentally harmful, but are at its mercy because they cannot see an exit. The thought of quitting would deeply disappoint all the external forces that shaped them, and those voices have literally become the breath in their lungs and the beats in their heart. Walking away from that would perhaps be tantamount to rejecting the basic needs for life. It is clear to see how this situation creates the perfect storm.

For the athletes who recognize their intense suffering, feel trapped in their circumstance, and who desperately want to heal from this brokenness, it is my belief that these individuals are exactly where God wants them.  I know that may not make sense because God does not want us to perpetually suffer.  That is not His plan for any of us.  However, suffering is usually always necessary for Him to be able to begin to heal anyone.  Athlete or not.

With that said, allow me to be the first to introduce to you that God has brought you here.  He has allowed you to endure the pain along with your success, and he has had His hand on you all along.  He loves you beyond what you can imagine, and He has incredible plans for your future.  Those plans may or may not involve athletics, but it is a certainty that these challenges and difficult moments will be used to help you in ways you cannot see right now.  Perhaps, the greater amount of hardship and suffering a person endures has a direct correlation to the incredible plan He has for your life.  He just desires that you are in a place where you *need* to seek Him so that He can help you achieve what His purpose is for you.

Remember discussing the basic agriculture cycle at the beginning of this book?  How the grain of wheat requires the soil to be tilled and broken in order for it to be able to take root, grow, and develop?  Well, I will offer to you that your state of brokenness has allowed God to enter your life, take root, and begin to grow inside you.  He was sitting there all along just waiting for the opportunity for you to intentionally plant Him so that He can help you recognize the strangling weeds and begin to eliminate them so that you can start the process of genuine healing that you are desperately seeking.

This is perhaps the most beautiful moment in your life and it comes at a time where you feel you are drowning in darkness and cannot see a way out. God *is* the light that will lead you out of these waters. He is the true source of healing, and you have just grabbed His hand that has been extended to you all along.

For some, this moment might be difficult to believe because perhaps God has been perceived as angry, judgmental, controlling, and the cause of tragedy and suffering. I will make an attempt at introducing you to who He really is despite what you might have been told or what you might think.

*God is love.*

Many of us have heard that and completely dismissed it as a silly, catchy, and possibly manipulative saying. It can be perceived that way especially if we have our own thoughts and ideas about God that do not line up with that assertion.

I will explain His love and what it looks like.

It is not a drive-up window with a menu of options and an immediate fulfillment of your order.

His love is the true *demonstration* of that word, which means that it is patient, kind, does not envy, does not boast, is not proud, does not dishonor, is not self-seeking, not easily angered, keeps no record of wrongs, does not delight in evil, but rejoices in truth. Love protects, trusts, hopes and always perseveres.

If that sounds familiar, I am sure you have heard it spoken at weddings many times. It is a summary of scripture taken straight out of the bible and is intended to infuse these truths into the hearts of the couple getting married. But this applies to you as well, because remember God is love, so these are all features that reflect him, and He will share them freely with you.

All that to say, if you truly want to begin to understand God, I encourage you to begin to see Him in these ways rather than any ideas you might have had that do not line up with these characteristics.

*"Love is patient, love is kind. It does not envy, it does not boast, it is not proud. It does not dishonor others, it is not self-seeking, it is not easily angered, it keeps no record of wrongs. Love does not delight in evil but rejoices with the truth. It always protects, always trusts, always hopes, always perseveres" 1 Corinthians 13:4-8 NIV*

With that, I will offer that God has been patiently waiting for you to seek Him. If you feel broken and lost, chances are that you are reaching out to Him. I assure you He is there and that you have found Him.

*"But without faith it is impossible to please Him, for he who comes to God must believe that He is, and that He is a rewarder of those who diligently seek Him" Hebrews 11:6 NKJV*

I believe it is safe to say that when people are doing well, experience no hardship, endure little suffering, and have perceived success they don't consider pursuing God. That makes sense because when things are going well, we inherently believe that we are doing things right and don't really even consider a need for God. If we don't consider a need for God, why would we seek Him?

That is precisely why a state of brokenness, although excruciating, is really a beautiful gift because it has put you in a place of needing to seek God. It has put you on a path where you have found Him, and it has intersected your life with His plan and purpose for you.

There is no greater gift than what you have just received. And the reward will far exceed any trophy, championship victory, or all-everything selections you have ever accomplished.

# Chapter 6

# The Opponent

Let's take a deeper dive into the weeds for a moment. Not to spend a lot of time on them, but as an athlete you clearly know and understand that there is an opponent. Without an opponent, well, would we even have sports? No.

You are also very aware that you, your teammates, and your coaches have spent a considerable amount of time examining your opponents and strategizing ways to claim victory over them. Significant time is spent analyzing the strengths, weaknesses, executions, plays, and strategies of your opponent all in an effort to understand them so the fight against them can be precise and effective. The purpose of this is to win the battle, the game, the match, the tournament, and the ultimate championship.

Nothing stated in that assertion causes an athlete to disagree. It is a fundamental truth. Sports are competitive and the ultimate outcome is to win. No argument there.

Clearly, within this very obvious truth, the strategies of the enemy are crucial to understand and be aware of. No coach would ever send their team into a game without preparation. A big part of this preparation involves understanding the opponent so that the performance of their team can put up an effective fight and win the game.

Application of this truth applies spiritually as well.

We all know that God is not manifested in the physical. He is a spiritual being that we all know, at some level, exists. If we all didn't know this at some level, why is there either belief, rejection, anger, reverence, or such disdain? We don't have those reactions to oxygen. We can't visually see oxygen, but obviously it is present. We know we need it, so I don't know of anyone furious at air, cursing at it, refusing to receive it, or unaware of its value. Since we all understand its importance, we have faith that it will be there for us and help us optimally function.

Again, that is a physical law. A physical truth. We recognize it and accept it even though we can't see it.

Since God is spiritual, we have to again, apply the natural law to the spiritual in this situation as well.

We all need God. But many of us do not comprehend this because He is not visible. Yet, we are suffering the consequences of His absence and are likely very unaware.

Well, God has an enemy, and this enemy is also *your* enemy.

This *is* the opponent you are up against and cannot recognize. It is the opponent that has taken root in your heart and has begun to produce its toxicity in your life. It is the opponent that has attempted to consume all the nutrients you have provided, and it has matured and demanded more and more from you at the expense of your value, identity, and worth.

At the risk of sounding dramatic, there is an enemy of your soul, and this enemy will take on any and all strategies to keep you blinded to him and convince you of literally anything so that you do not seek God. This enemy is Satan. He is a spirit that you can't see and he knows that God is your only hope for victory over him. He will continue to show up in your life as a weed and take all the food, water, and nutrients you throw at him and hope he is never exposed for who he is.

Perhaps this is difficult to believe, but I assure you, that just because you may not necessarily believe this is true, it is literally the only battle in your life that you must be victorious over. It is the only game in your life that you need to win. It is the only race in your life that matters.

He is your opponent, and it is time you receive revelation of his strategies and their toxic manifestations in your life so that you can defeat him and claim victory over his deceptive, cunning, manipulative plans for you.

*"For we do not wrestle against flesh and blood, but against principalities, against powers, against the rulers of the darkness of this age, against spiritual hosts of wickedness in the heavenly places" Ephesians 6:12 NKJV*

Please read that again. No battle, struggle, fight, or war in our lives is between people (flesh and blood). It is between powers and spiritual hosts. That means that the hell you have been in has been caused by these spiritual forces of wickedness. You were not aware of that, so you have not been able to effectively battle and conquer them.

As we have learned, no athlete goes into a game or match without having prepared or studied their opponent. If they were to do that, it doesn't take a genius to figure out that they will not win. They will be defeated...easily.

We all live in a physical body and it serves as a host for our spirit and soul. Our spirit is the essence of who we are. It is our personality, our consciousness, our energy. It is also eternal, unlike our physical bodies. So, this opponent (Satan) does not care if you win or lose a game, he does not care if you are All-Conference, All-State, All-American, or All-Universe. Those are not his battles and he could truly care less about your athletic success.

What he does care about, is keeping you focused on those things in any way possible, so that you do not ever seek God. Why is that? God is his ultimate enemy, and he is using *you* to attempt to defeat God by winning your spirit. Your spirit is involved in the ultimate battle between God and Satan.

*Your spirit is involved in the ultimate battle between God and Satan.*

There are countless manipulative tactics Satan uses in this battle, but in the case of the athlete, he seems to frequently use external sources and voices to shape the mind and heart of a young, impressionable child. When athletic success is discovered, the accolades and personal successes naturally ensue. Again, this is not necessarily negative, however, when it continues in such a way that the athlete is seeking, responding to, watching for, and behaving in accordance with those external voices, then that becomes the trap. In this situation, the athlete is seeking approval and guidance from others. Not God.

This is a dangerous and cunning deception, and it starts early so it is extremely difficult to recognize and even more difficult to break. If the athlete is so entangled in the approval of others, no wonder they don't consider seeking God because they are seeking approval from everyone else around them.

Sadly, if the athlete never realizes this, and continues in this same cycle, their spirit belongs to the enemy because God was never pursued.  Patterns like this don't just go away, they often continue well past high school, college, or even professional athletic levels. It is precisely why it is so critical to understand this as early as possible so that you can begin to properly compete and easily overcome this deceptive enemy.

But you cannot *ever* overcome him without God.  It is impossible.

What is even more amazing, is that with God, there is literally no performance, no perfection, no strategy, no plan necessary to find Him.  It is the opposite of what you have been living your entire life, and it requires nothing of you except faith and belief.  I will discuss this further in a later chapter, but just that alone should eliminate some pressure from you because you do not have to work or perform to earn God's approval.  Honestly, you literally can't perform for Him.  He is not looking for your effort, talent, or good behavior.  He is looking for your spirit and soul because He loves *you*.  Not your accomplishments.

# Chapter 7

# Defeated

We have spent some time revealing the true opponent, or enemy of your life. We have discovered how he operates and deceives so that you don't think about or consider pursuing God. Let's tap into your competitive instincts here and talk about eliminating the power you have unwittingly provided to your own personal enemy.

But first, please don't be hard on yourself because it happens to all of us. You are no different, even though your experiences might be unique to you. Satan will manifest himself in to the lives of everyone and exploit weaknesses, blind spots, and frankly, our ignorance of God.

If I may be so bold to suggest that our ignorance of God, is the only opening that the enemy needs in order to plant his seeds and then sit back and allow us to innocently water and care for them as they develop and grow in your life. In your situation, perhaps the enemy knows that you do not know God, His truth, His weapons, or His promises so frankly he has seen you as his ally, not necessarily his opponent.

But that is about to change, and now he has not only realized that the spirit of God has been invited in by you, he also realizes that the spirit of God has entered into a highly driven, deeply competitive, and powerfully motivated individual.  I can't wait to tell you how much authority you have right now and how little power the enemy truly has in your life.

This is perhaps where the incredible "birth" of your life's purpose begins.

I want to be clear.  You have an incredible life purpose in the eyes of God.  He is sovereign, which means he is in control of everything. His sovereignty is so magnificent and omnipotent, that it allows us to have free-will.  He can operate and orchestrate everything beyond the parameters of our choices and decisions, and then somehow use them for our own benefit.  That might sound too difficult to comprehend, and yes, I agree, there is complexity involved that is far too superior for our finite human minds to grasp.  However, please hear and receive His promise to all of us. Even our own ignorant, bad, poor, and self-destructive choices and decisions can and will be used in God's plan for our lives.  This is a promise!

*"And we know that all things work together for good to those who love God, to those who are called according to His purpose" Romans 8:28 NKJV*

Perhaps you have read that scripture before and that it has positively affected you in some way.  After understanding that you have likely spent your life nurturing the weeds planted by the enemy, you might be wondering how this could apply to you.

God, in His sovereign wisdom, knows you.  He knows your personality, your internal drive, your competitiveness, your fierce countenance, and your inherent desire to overcome and win battles.  Maybe, just maybe, he has allowed these traits and characteristics to develop in you so that He can steer you into the plans He has for you. Plans for your good and for His glory.

God needs warriors because, as you have learned, this battle is fierce and it is serious. You need to understand that you have been chosen, hand selected, and prepared to be a leader for Him. What an honor and privilege! You don't have to stress about performance, statistics, or even winning. With God, the battle has already been won and the enemy has been defeated.

*"I have said these things to you, that in me you may have peace. In the world you will have tribulation. But take heart; I have overcome the world" John 16:33 ESV*

*"But thanks be to God, who gives us the victory through our Lord Jesus Christ" 1 Corinthians 15:57 ESV*

*"He disarmed the rulers and authorities and put them to open shame, by triumphing over them in him" Colossians 2:15 ESV*

*"Have I not commanded you? Be strong and courageous. Do not be frightened, and do not be dismayed, for the Lord your God is with you wherever you go" Joshua 1:9 ESV*

*"No, in all these things we are more than conquerors through him who loved us. For I am sure that neither death nor life, nor angels nor rulers, nor things present nor things to come, nor powers, nor height nor depth, nor anything else in all creation, will be able to separate us from the love of God in Christ Jesus our Lord" Romans 8:37-39 ESV*

So, here we go.

In the beginning of this book, you read through the introduction, and you prayed to invite God into your life, and you believed upon Jesus Christ and that He paid the penalty for your imperfections, bad choices, and areas that you have fallen short. If you did that with sincerity, then you not only have received eternal salvation, but you have also armed yourself with all the power and authority of the universe. This intentional decision on your part has now assured victory over your greatest enemy.

It. Is. Finished.

That amazing story will be discussed toward the end of this book, but for now, just know and have confidence that you have the spirit of God within you, and that you are sealed until the day of redemption! Not only do you have this assurance, but you also have the *only* weapon that can battle, conquer, and defeat the enemy of your soul.

You have been a part of the 2% in athletics. Welcome to the 2% in the Kingdom of God.

The next few chapters will help you understand your life moving forward. Clearly, there is no way of projecting where it will go, or what will happen. Be aware that you may experience the same ups and downs with your athletic career as you always have. But I want you to remember that athletics are only a vehicle by which God plans to launch and propel you. Like your enemy, He doesn't focus on your performance, batting average, Personal Record, or conference standings. No. God looks far deeper than those things and although they are not His focus, He still cares about you and He still wants you to do the best that you can in whatever you are engaged in. If that is your athletics at the moment, then He cares!

When He created you, He created an amazing individual whom He has called to do incredible things. He gifted you with tremendous athletic ability, so He knows and desires that you pursue your athletic talent. His intention for your athletic ability may surface during your athletic career. It may not surface until your sports are well behind you. Only God can answer that. However, I would begin to pay attention to this calling upon your life and begin to pray about God's purpose for it.  To be honest, your purpose has already been set in motion and will be completely fulfilled in His time.  It may be on a grand scale, it may be a series of subtle expressions, or it may be a life filled with serving others.  Whatever it is, He is now able to lead you in that direction, and it is immensely important.

It is also vital to understand, now that God is in your life, is that He will begin to shift your focus to align with His.  For some, this may happen right away, but for many, it will take time.  There is no way to determine how this unfolds in the lives of athletes because God's plan is always very unique and specific to each person.  Please know that if the spirit of God *truly* resides within you, that your life will begin to reflect Him.

This does not mean that you will become perfect.  This does not mean that you will stop making mistakes.  This does not mean that you will never fall short again.  This means that you will continue to do all these things because you are human and live in an imperfect body of flesh like all of us.  However, your spirit will become innocent and pure in the sight of the Lord because He will see you through His perfect son, Jesus Christ.  And Jesus will be your constant advocate against every single accusation and claim hurled by the enemy of your soul.

He has just been defeated and will remain defeated no matter what life throws at you.

# Chapter 8

# The Gift

We live in a society where performance plays a significant role in our success and our accomplishments. It really doesn't matter if you are an athlete or working in a job in your particular career field. This is a reality that we are all familiar with no matter where we are in life.

For the athlete, this reality is not only quite real from a societal perspective, but it is significantly amplified from an athletic perspective. Honestly, there is no way to extract or remove performance from the mind, emotion, or physical traits of the athlete. You simply can't and expect them to remain an athlete.

This book is not intended to criticize or disparage the pursuit of excellence, top performance, or distinction. For a variety of reasons, the flesh is designed to strive for these goals in whatever areas we find motivation. If these pursuits, combined with the power of God, are within us, then there is no ceiling and there are no limits to the profound impact available at our fingertips.

Without God, these pursuits will provide only temporal satisfaction and immediate gratification to the individual. Any and all efforts without God, no matter how noble, is basically just a weed that will get burned, separated, and disposed of at the end. That is a fact and a truth that cannot be undone because it only has a physical life, not a spiritual one. Remember, the physical dies.  The spiritual is eternal.

In the previous chapter we talked about no longer needing to stress about performance, statistics, or even winning now that you are a believer.  That may not sound realistic at all, so let's break things down even more so that there is clarity on what that means.

When a person becomes a believer, they invite the spirit of God into their lives.  They are "born again" in the spirit and that means they have the Holy Spirit now indwelling them.  When the spirit of God lives within a person, it lives within the body (host) of the person.

The body is physical and made up of flesh.  We all understand that.

The flesh is purely self-centered.  It requires attention from every aspect in order to keep it temporarily satisfied.  Its appetite becomes greater and greater and more demanding once it has achieved what it set out to achieve.  The physical body needs water, food, attention, praise, accolades, control, power, accomplishment. You name it.

I know that sounds really awful when you look at it that way, but we all live in our bodies and we all experience the selfish demands of our bodies.  It is a natural way of life.  We can't help that fact and God knows it.  That is precisely why He wants to connect His spirit with our spirit.  When we pass on from this life, our flesh does not go anywhere.  It literally dies, decomposes, and forever remains in its final resting place.

The spirit, as previously described, is eternal.  It goes on living well past our physical death. When our spirit is sealed with the Holy Spirit (or spirit of God), then its eternal destiny is with God.

*"In Him you also trusted, after you heard the word of truth, the gospel of your salvation; in whom also, having believed, you were sealed with the Holy Spirit of promise, who is the guarantee of our inheritance until the redemption of the purchased possession, to the praise of His glory" Ephesians 1:13-14*

The spirit of God is in direct opposition to the flesh. The spirit of God is not self-centered or demanding, and the two will forever be at odds with each other moving forward. This will cause some conviction and internal struggles from time to time, but when that happens, allow it to give you confidence that God is within you and is gently guiding you...not forcing you to be perfect or to perform somehow to keep your salvation. It is gentle guidance to encourage you to make decisions that will be beneficial for you and bring honor and glory to Him. He understands you will make mistakes and not always make decisions that will produce this outcome, but know and trust that you are sealed. He is not going to remove Himself from you. He will NOT abandon you. Perhaps two of the most hopeful, secure, and blessed promises in the Bible are these:

*"What then shall we say to these things? If God is for us, who can be against us? He who did not spare His own Son, but delivered Him up for us all, how shall He not with Him also freely give us all things? Who shall bring a charge against God's elect? It is God who justifies. Who is he who condemns? It is Christ who died, and furthermore is also risen, who is even at the right hand of God, who also makes intercession for us. Who shall separate us from the love of Christ? Shall tribulation, or distress, or persecution, or famine, or nakedness, or peril, or sword? As it is written:*

*For Your sake we are killed all day long;*

*We are accounted as sheep for the slaughter.*

*Yet in all these things we are more than conquerors through Him who loved us. For I am persuaded that neither death nor life, nor angels nor principalities nor powers, nor things present nor things to come, nor height nor depth, nor any other created thing, shall be able to separate us from the love of God which is in Christ Jesus our Lord"* Romans 8:31-39 NKJV

*"For God did not send His Son into the world to condemn the world, but that the world through Him might be saved"* John 3:17 NKJV

So, with those promises, you can now breathe easy that the ultimate battle, fight, race, and war has been won and you can't do one thing to mess it up. What a gift!

Speaking of gifts, salvation is just that. It has nothing to do with your performance as a person, athlete, church parishioner, volunteer work, or any level of perfection you might have been striving for. The days of relentlessly performing to accomplish approval from God is over. When you realize that you can't work for His approval, the pressure is off and the receiving of this gift will become a deeply valued and treasured possession within you.

The next chapter will discuss how to detangle the performance-based mentality that you have developed as an athlete and keep it in its proper lane and not apply it to your spiritual standing with God. It will be difficult, but God understands this and will be extremely patient as He matures you from a spiritual infant, into a mature believer. This will not happen overnight. Just as physical development does not happen overnight. It is a process and you are now on the right path.

*"For the wages of sin is death; but the gift of God is eternal life through Jesus Christ our Lord"* Romans 6:23 KJV

It's a gift.

# Chapter 9

# Identity

I understand that was a lot of perhaps what you might refer to as "preaching". However, I want to make sure you recognize the biblical basis for any teaching and analogy used in this book, so that you don't think it is just some random idea. It is very important that you know that these messages are based on God's principles, promises, and truth. Everything else is just rhetoric, opinions, and empty persuasions. Those things can only offer you hollow text and perhaps another carrot to keep you turning in the dizzying vortex you have been in for so long.

Back to the weeds.

Yes. The weeds have grown prolifically while you have been diligently watering them. They have grown and matured to the point that they are producing their poisonous fruit and causing you significant torment and trauma. If you are reading this book, I am certain you are swimming in your own sea of desperation. You are secretly suffering and wondering how you can get the anxiety, the pressure, the depression, and the overwhelming stress to subside.

Being an athlete requires you to always be on your top game. There is no place for mediocrity, apathy, or indifference because if these were to somehow enter into your athletic circle, you would be benched, replaced, or never get to see the court or the field at all. It is a private suffering and you do all you can to find ways in the natural to combat these dark forces. All in an effort to take the edge off or to help you feel good in a momentary period of time.

Now we need to discuss how we can begin to reduce these weeds and start to kill them off. There is really only one way to do that, and you have already taken the most important step. Be advised that the enemy is not going to un-plant his seeds and weeds. It will require a little strategy from you, but just know that if you begin to water and nurture what God says about you and not what others are saying about you, then the weeds will begin to wither and eventually die.

It makes a lot of sense!

But first you need to know what God says about you, what He thinks of you, and how He sees you. This is the wheat that you just planted in your broken soil, and now need to cultivate and nurture it! It will grow alongside the weeds, but eventually, if you continue to take care of it, the roots will begin to deepen and eventually consume the space that was once occupied by the fake counterpart.

God, the authentic wheat, will mature and produce grain that is useful, nutritious, and can ultimately serve hundreds of thousands of lives. It is a source of nutrition that when harvested, can feed countless individuals. You can see its benefit and how it reaches well beyond you.

So, what does God say about you? If you are going to nurture the wheat, the authentic seed...what will it produce?

First and foremost, you are now a child of God. Although many people want to say we are all God's children, that is sadly mistaken.

Only individuals who believe that Jesus paid the penalty for their shortcomings and imperfections are considered a child of God.

There is your identity.

For so long, your identity has been you as the athlete.  It has fit in some ways, but you have still felt lost and in some dark void that has not allowed you to truly grasp who you are.  I will say that my identity was so lost for the longest time.  I often wondered who I was and why I was even here.  I truly wondered about that often and never understood who I was.  I never had an identity to speak of.  This feeling was very troubling and often created terrible confusion in my life because I was always in search of it.

Without a question, one of the most profound and emotionally beautiful moments I have ever experienced, was when God allowed me to understand who I was.  I instantly knew my identity for the first time ever and I was well into my 30's.  It was a miracle and it solidified my existence immediately when I realized it.

God had allowed me to go through tremendous suffering and trials.  Perhaps similar in ways you are experiencing now.  Feelings of hopelessness, severe anxiety, feeling lost, and deep despair consumed my life and I had no way of getting myself out of that.

But as I reached to God for help...He answered in more profound ways than I could have ever imagined.  He first helped me understand my identity.  An incredibly powerful moment for me and I trust will be for you too.  His words spoke directly to me and revealed who I was.

*"If you endure chastening, God deals with you as with sons; for what son is there whom a father does not chasten? But if you are without chastening, of which all have become partakers, then you are illegitimate and not sons" Hebrews 12:7-8 NKJV*

So, for me, I knew my suffering was allowed by God, and I knew it was a form of chastening, or discipline. But once I recognized that, I also recognized that God disciplines HIS children. The scripture is clear that He does not discipline anyone who is not His child. This reveals who you are.

You are a child of God.

That is your identity. Not the stellar volleyball player, not the MVP quarterback, not the track star, not the greatest pitcher in the conference.

A child of God.

You are also a new creation. The moment you believed; you were instantly transformed. When you believed that Jesus died for you, you were repentant. Repent means to change your mind. You went from unbelief to belief, so now all of your transgressions have been covered by the blood and sacrifice of Jesus Christ. If you don't have any deeper understanding of this right now, it is ok. There is time for that and God will reveal it to you. It is just important that you have chosen to believe that Jesus died, was buried, and resurrected to account for your sins and shortcomings. He did that for the entire world, but many choose to reject it. Those who reject it will have to pay their own penalty. You don't want any part of that. Trust me.

 So, you now know your identity as a child of God and you are also a new creation.

*"Therefore, if anyone is in Christ, he is a new creation; old things have passed away; behold, all things have become new" 2 Corinthians 5:17*

I am not sure that there can be any more joy infused as you become aware of these truths. Just this knowledge imparts tremendous power and authority into your life. The realization of these promises instantly stands you on solid ground and provides a sense of security, protection, and refuge.  Perhaps sensations that have been absent until now.  But know that this is the authentic seed taking root and establishing its firm foundation within you.

That is powerful.

# Chapter 10

# Construction

We have all heard the saying "fruit of our labor". It is a common saying that people use when they start a project and can't truly see or appreciate it until its completion. The fruit is the outcome of said hard work. Again, the analogy is comparable to performance because it requires hard "work" to be able to enjoy the fruits of the labor.

It's not necessarily a bad thing because if someone is going to build a house, they have to start at the foundation and work hard to construct it, assemble the infrastructure, and involve plenty of muscle in getting it complete. But what an amazing creation from all the hard work that went into it. Without question, it also looked incredibly messy until it was finished. Once again, a law of nature that we all recognize and comprehend, and a necessary labor of love to produce.

The most amazing spiritual analogy in this scenario is that there will be a beautiful construction, infrastructure, and labor of love effort put into you as well. Since you are now a new creation, as shared in the previous chapter, your life will now begin to build on the new foundation which has been laid.

Each element of construction will be carefully assembled. The energy source will be wisely engineered, and the building materials will be hand selected to ensure protection from the harsh winds and perilous storms that will come against it.

At the end of this process, will be not a house…. but a temple.

Yes. That's right. When God enters into your life, his spirit cannot dwell in a natural state of existence. It must reside in the most glorious space there is. He declares that as a temple, and so His labor of love begins.

You read that correctly. It is HIS labor that begins. Not yours. So, the performance of this process does not rest on you, but on Him. As your new life is being constructed, please realize this and understand that it will get messy at times, and it will seem incomplete to you. However, God does not operate in anything less than perfect, and this state of perfection will be accomplished, I assure you. But that perfection will not be realized until we enter into heaven. In the meantime, God will be hard at work building the most beautiful temple for Him to reside, and you can have that comfort and knowledge that He is the architect, construction crew, and Superintendent of your supernatural temple.

Now the other fruit. Your temple is the fruit of God's labor, but He also wants to produce healthy, beautiful, nutritious, and beneficial fruit in you. He does not want the weeds to consume the inside of His temple, so He will begin to help you identify the grains of wheat that have been planted so that you can nurture that instead of the toxic thorns you have been watering all along.

Here is where it can get sticky for some people because they have been conditioned and programmed to listen to the weeds telling them to "do this", "act like that", "perform for the critics", "try to get coach Smith to like you", "If I hit a homerun, Dad will finally be proud".

Any number of thoughts that might enter your mind as an athlete in order to perform to achieve approval from other people. That is likely the athletic environment in which you have grown up in, so it has become so engrained in every aspect of your life, thought process, and behavior.

This will now start its process of changing, and again, it will be a process so allow yourself some grace. We will walk through powerful ways in which this can begin to change and that you can develop and cultivate the healthy and authentic seeds that have now been planted within you.

Now you need to see yourself as a glorious temple and not just a decaying body. What an amazing start! Yes. That JUST happened.

Next, we need to understand what the fruits of God are. Without knowing what this is, we will fill in the blanks with our own natural understanding, and I can assure you that we will fill in performance-based outcomes and "works" that we think we will need to achieve in order to gain the approval of God.

Please hear me. That is not accurate. Your approval in the eyes of God has been secured and you do NOT have to do one thing to try to sustain it. I will go into that in more detail, however, your days of striving for approval are over.

So, what are the fruits of God's spirit?

*"But the fruit of the Spirit is love, joy, peace, longsuffering, kindness, goodness, faithfulness, gentleness, self-control. Against such there is no law. And those who are Christ's have crucified the flesh with its passions and desires" Galatians 5:22-24*

Please read that again, and begin to absorb this truth as you may experience intense opposition to this moving forward. Your flesh will try to get in the way, external voices may try to convince you that you have to work hard and perform to sustain your salvation, and you have to do all kinds of work for the church in order to be accounted worthy.

None of that is true. In fact, these are the weeds that are still trying to have a place in your life and get you to water them. God knows who you are and He has accepted you completely because He loves you immensely. He knows you are imperfect. It is why He died for you. He knows that. But now that He is residing within you, He will guide and work through you.

The *exact* opposite of what you have always known.

Does that mean you won't be of service to God? No. It means that God has gifted you with certain talents, aptitudes, and gifts. You already have those as a part of your DNA, your hearts desires, and your natural talents. He made you that way. He will inspire you to activate those talents and gifts. As He does this, you will be fulfilling your purpose! You may not even realize it, but He is the energy source in your temple, and He will energize you in the areas that He created for you. As you do this, your purpose on this earth will become more and more defined and you will realize one day, what He created you for and you will see How God has used you to fulfill His will through you.

You have a most high calling on your life.

As we examine and inspect the fruit more deeply, I want to be very clear that the fruit of the spirit is truly God at work in you. It is NOT and frankly CANNOT be you. That truth should allow you to rest and enjoy some peace that perhaps you have not experienced. You may hear others say that the scripture used to identify the fruit of the spirit forces you to "crucify the flesh". That part of the scripture seems to get twisted in the minds of people because it infers that WE have to CRUCIFY the flesh. That suggests that we have to work, struggle, perform, and strive to accomplish this.

It took me a long time to grasp what God was saying in this passage. But His Word makes it very clear to understand that not one human can ever crucify the flesh. It is impossible. If it were possible for a person to do this, God would not have sent His son Jesus, to be CRUCIFIED for the flesh.

So, the scripture is clear when reading it that it requires crucifixion to overcome the flesh. Only one has been crucified and that is Jesus Christ, and He has been crucified for that very thing. No one else has been or can be.

The other truth that must be shared here is that our own work, our own effort, and our own performance is truly viewed as rubbish. When we do things in our own will and through our own performance in order to seek approval for our "good deeds" or attempts at righteousness, we are offering up filth in the eyes of God. I know that sounds harsh, but allow me to explain. But first, don't take my word for it.

*"But we are all like an unclean thing, and all our righteousness are like filthy rags; We all fade as a leaf, and our iniquities, like the wind, have taken us away" Isaiah 64:6 NKJV*

If this discourages you, allow me to help you view it through the eyes of God. This truth should take the burden and pressure off of you and allow the Holy Spirit of God to do the work for you. That is likely very foreign and difficult to comprehend, but just knowing that should help remove some of the jolting anxiety that has been coursing through your body for so long.

Finally, I want to help offer you confidence that the work to be completed in you will not be of your own effort, but will be of God. It is His responsibility and His work.

*"For we are His workmanship, created in Christ Jesus for good works, which God prepared beforehand that we should walk in them"* Ephesians 2:10 NKJV

*"Being confident of this very thing, that He who has begun a good work in you will complete it until the day of Jesus Christ"* Philippians 1:6

*"For he who has entered His rest has himself also ceased from his works as God did from His"* Hebrews 4:10 NKJV

There are countless other scriptures that speak to the Lord performing the works in you, and if you are truly His child, then he will produce those works because He also declares that faith without works is dead.

*"Thus, also faith by itself, if it does not have works, is dead"* James 2:17

Clearly, faith is essential.  However, your faith was activated when you believed in Jesus.  The works, as just described and supported in scripture, is God.  He has equipped you, and walked the path ahead of you to do this work in you.  It does not mean that you have to prove yourself to anyone to demonstrate your salvation to any man.  Those days are over and that is not biblical.

God wants you to rest in Him and allow *Him* to begin to produce the fruit (do the work) that He promises.

# Chapter 11

# Fruit

Now that the foundation has been laid and the construction started, it is time to compare the fruit of the authentic against the weeds.  We will be comparing the fruit of the spirit against the fruit of the enemy.  They are opposing forces and they produce opposite manifestations within you.

We spent a few chapters discussing the weeds and their toxic effects in your life.  Below is a side-by-side comparison to help you distinguish them through a concrete view.

| FRUIT OF THE ENEMY | FRUIT OF THE HOLY SPIRIT |
| --- | --- |
| Depression | Joy |
| Anxiety | Peace |
| Impatience | Longsuffering |
| Hatred | Kindness |
| Evil | Goodness |
| Disloyalty | Faithfulness |
| Hardness | Gentleness |
| Self-Indulgence | Self-control |

You can see by the comparison of the fruit, that both forces are not necessarily focusing on your sport or athleticism, but both want to utilize your God-given talent to work in you, to produce the ultimate manifestation of their seed.

Your athletic talent just happens to be a vehicle they can use to nurture and develop their purpose in your life. As you can see their purpose is in direct opposition, and reflective of the characteristics of the seeds that have been planted.

You can also clearly see how the entirety of the "performance" culture has likely created some of these outcomes, which is perhaps why you are reading this book.

As an athlete, you may think these outcomes are not going to help your statistics, positioning on the team, or performance on the court. However, I would strongly encourage you to reconsider.

How many times have you heard someone refer to you or another athlete's performance being adversely affected because they are "mental". It happens all the time. That term or phrase is well known in the athletic community as the pressures of performance wreaking havoc on natural talent. When an athlete is "mental" they clearly aren't performing well and are affected by these mental pressures.

As you likely know, these mental states are not simply present during the game. They come home with you and keep you up at night. They tear you down and rip you to shreds. They eat away at your core and they bring dark messages of defeat and unworthiness. A ferocious cycle that can grow and strengthen until it becomes so convincing that the athlete starts to assume these lies as their personal truth. The downward spiral of this belief system has likely brought you to this place of brokenness. A place that feels ominous and devoid of hope.

Well let me assure you, you are in the exact place you should be, because as we have learned in earlier chapters, that what the enemy means for evil, God can use for good.  That includes this difficult, seemingly impossible place that you are in right now.

*"As for you, you meant evil against me, but God meant it for good"*
*Genesis 50:20*

As mentioned, the enemy is not going to "un-plant" his weeds, so there are essentially two ways that you can begin to activate God in your life to help you begin to pull them, eliminate them, and overcome them.

One way is to understand how God sees you and begin to nurture that.  The other way is to utilize the supernatural weapons that God has now equipped you with to help remove the weeds and prevent new one's from attempting to find a place in your heart (fertile soil).

Be aware that there will always be weeds, but you will now understand how to recognize most of them, and effectively address them. In the end, the weeds that grow alongside the authentic wheat, that look almost identical, will be addressed directly by God. You will likely not be able to discern this look-alike, but He can.  He also knows this weed cannot be removed until the harvest and there is a very specific way to remove it.  We will discuss this at the end of the book.

In the meantime, there is a lot you can do.

First, it is imperative that you begin to understand how God sees you.

He loves you immensely, and He loves you as you are.  All your flaws, imperfections, talents, gifts, and mistakes.  He does not look at what you have or haven't done.  He loves YOU.  That is difficult for all of us to truly grasp because we haven't experienced that kind of unconditional love on this earth. Even if we have been loved by people in these genuine ways, it does not and cannot compare to this kind of pure, unconditional, and all-consuming love.

He views you as wonderfully and fearfully made. In all your personal views of yourself and your perceived understanding of how others see you, it is vital that you know that God has wonderfully and fearfully made you. You can begin to let go of the performance expectations, the moving targets, the bar that gets raised, the personal best you have to beat, the impossible accomplishments that the external voices are demanding of you.

If you walk off the field with a .000 batting average, hit the ball into the net 15 times, throw 6 interceptions, scratch on each jump or throw, or don't make the all-star team, you are still in God's favor and you are still as valuable to Him as you were when you produced the amazing athletic statistics you and others were striving to see you achieve. Your value is NOT connected to your athletic performance. Not ever.

Allow this truth to absorb into your mind. It may be extremely difficult or even foreign for some because perhaps you have suffered abuse, neglect, or even a deeply legalistic, religious upbringing. All of these environments can and tend to produce approval-seeking behavior in people because it engenders a feeling of unworthiness which can generate a deep-seeded propensity to perform in order to gain approval and acceptance. For others, this environment can produce rebellious behaviors and tendencies as a reaction to living in a perceived impossible environment.

Either way, these are seeds planted by the enemy intended to confuse you and distract you from understanding how God really sees you. We naturally assume that God is the same as the forces in our environment. This happens to almost everyone, and it blinds us from truth. We then believe this crafty deception that the enemy has used. Sadly, this keeps many away from God because they can't see Him through all the toxic weeds that have been prolifically growing in their lives.

But God....

God wants you to start to recognize His voice. He will begin to gently speak to you and share His truth with you. His truth is vastly different than anything in the natural, but it is all-powerful and able to penetrate lies and deception as if it were a fierce and divisive sword. His truth does not have to be demanded because it can stand on itself. And in all things, authentic truth, when pursued, prevails.

Remember earlier when we talked about how the mind is the ground and the heart is the soil in your life. One of the ways in which God's truth can be nurtured is to understand it and then feed it. As you do this, you are actually beginning to mature your spirit. When your spirit matures, it takes over the soil in your heart and absorbs the nutrients you provide.

The more you do this, the less space there is for the weeds of the enemy. The root of God will reach deeper and deeper into your life and begin to replace the poisonous barbs and thorns and eventually root them out. As this happens, you will notice that there is less and less of the anxiety, depression, and worthlessness and there will be more and more peace, joy, and self-control in your life.

God speaks to you and He will continue to speak to you, but it is important to recognize what He says and how He speaks. His words are always loving, encouraging, hopeful, and truthful. They are never condemning, abusive, demanding, or deceptive.

*"Finally, brethren, whatever things are true, whatever things are noble, whatever things are just, whatever things are pure, whatever things are lovely, whatever things are of good report, if there is any virtue and if there is anything praiseworthy— meditate on these things" Philippians 4:8*

If you receive a thought, or hear words that are in opposition to those things, know and trust they are not from God. That is different than receiving constructive criticism or a truth that might be difficult to hear from someone (i.e. an honest disagreement with someone you love or care about). We are not perfect individuals, so it is not always a negative thing to hear truth from someone even if it is painful to hear.

What I am talking about are thoughts and messages in your head that attempt to convince you that you are not good enough, not worthy of accomplishing things, not lovable, not valuable, or not (fill in the blank). Those repeat messages are NOT from God and they are intended to continue to destroy you.

The enemy has only three jobs. They are to STEAL, KILL, AND DESTROY.

Those messages, when allowed to continue, will accomplish their goal in your life, and you will realize one day that you were tricked into believing these things and it may be too late when you understand this. That is why it is important to understand the heart of God and to listen for His voice. As spoken clearly in the scripture, He speaks only things that are true, noble, pure, lovely and of good report. He wants you to meditate on all virtuous and praiseworthy things.

Meditate is another word for contemplate and strongly consider. In other words, give it more thought and focus and begin the process of rejecting any thoughts and messages of the contrary. It is extremely important that you do this because remember, what seed enters your mind (ground) will get planted in the soil (your heart) and take root.  Then it will grow.

These are the seeds that you want to take root and grow in you.

# Chapter 12

# Prevention

One way God will begin to eliminate the toxic poison from your life is by helping you recognize and hear His voice. Once you begin to do this and then allow His truth to enter your life, it will begin to overpower the useless weapons of the enemy.

The enemy has no power.  It can only operate by the permission that it is given - by you.  Now that you have the spirit of God, you literally have the power of the entire universe within you.  God has ultimate power and authority, and now you do as well because you can exercise His authority within you.

As we continue to pursue God and His truth, He will begin to take more space in your heart and as this happens, the space available for the enemy will become less and less.  This is one of the weapons that God has now equipped you with to combat the strangling, asphyxiating weeds that had been there for so long.

But be aware, the enemy is a relentless foe and will not give up his pursuit to steal, kill, and destroy the plans that God has for you.  He understands that God has incredible purpose for your life and that it will involve revealing the source of all good to others.  Satan does not want this, so he will continue his strategies against you.

As your heart becomes more and more filled with God, through hearing His voice, recognizing His language, and believing His words, the enemy will continue his attack with negative, dark, deceptive thoughts. Remember, he knows that the best way to influence you is through lies and deception, and this strategy has been effective for him. He will continue in this way because remember, Satan has no power. He only has cunning, vicious lies at his disposal. Truth is not in him, so he cannot and will not share truth with you.

His method is to get you to believe the lies in your mind and as we have talked about, those lies then enter your heart and then he gets the opportunity to grow in your life and influence you in a direction that you don't want to go.

So, you can see that it is essential for you to stop this attack in the thought process stage (seed on the ground). If you recognize his tactics early, you can prevent them from being planted in your heart (fertile soil) and then growing into full blown maturity.

God has exposed this strategy for you, and as a result, has equipped you with another effective weapon against the enemy of your soul.

*"For though we walk in the flesh, we do not war according to the flesh. For the weapons of our warfare are not carnal but mighty in God for pulling down strongholds, casting down arguments and every high thing that exalts itself against the knowledge of God, bringing every thought into captivity to the obedience of Christ" 2 Corinthians 10:3-5*

In these few scriptures, God tells us that our fight against this enemy is not to be conducted in the flesh. It is a spiritual war which requires the use of unconventional weapons. The weapon that God is equipping you with here is the identification of the enemy's thoughts that will continue to try to enter into your mind. God is letting you know this will happen, but that you have authority over those thoughts.

He is telling you that when you get assaulted with any thought that is dark, or exalts itself over God, or does not line up with the truth of God (that we have talked about in earlier chapters), then it is important to bring those thoughts into captivity (recognize them for what they are and who they are from) and reject them immediately.  As you reject them, you are understanding their source, you are remembering that God is within you, and then you are rejecting those thoughts.  The rejection of these thoughts exercises the authority that God has given you.

When you do this, you are actually fighting a raging war with the supernatural weapons that you need to prevail against this enemy. Again, this battle is not a "flesh and blood" battle.  It is, as God tells you, a spiritual war, and He is teaching you how to have victory over the ultimate father of lies.

Perhaps you are thinking to yourself, "this seems too easy".  When examining this process in theory, it does seem to be a simple fight. However, I encourage you to look back at the effectiveness of the strategy used.  These thoughts have come at you through a variety of voices and experiences and has perhaps caused you to respond to all those external judgements, criticisms, and exaltations, and those messages have been allowed entry into your heart.  Now you are suffering the consequences of all those lies being planted and taking life in your heart.

It is really the same life cycle of the natural, however, it must be applied to the spiritual as well.

God has now equipped you with two powerful weapons against the enemy and you can use your free-will to exercise them.  With the spirit of God residing within you, His authority comes with it.  So, the next time thoughts that enter your mind, cause you fear, anxiety, or stress, know that is the enemy and cancel the thoughts immediately by using God's authority.

Speak it out loud.  Say, "I cancel these thoughts right now in the authority of Jesus Christ." Whatever you have to say to exercise the authority you now have.  Repeat this as often as you need to and then pay attention.  Soon these thoughts will dissipate and begin to leave you.  It is important that you call out the source of the power (Jesus Christ) because you are using *His* authority.  Not your own. His name carries immense power and the enemy is required to flee and leave when His name is declared in a command.

Finally, as an athlete, you understand that is essential to adjust your game plan in order to claim victory over your opponent.  How do you know to adjust your gameplan?   By studying and understanding the tactics and strategies of your opponent.  This opponent happens to be an unseen, spiritual wrecking ball.

The amazing truth is that the weapons used against these forces are not of your own strength, from your talent, or within your physical prowess.  They are all of God.

You just need to execute them.

# Chapter 13

# The Ultimate Victory

With all the experience you have as an athlete, you know that all strategies used have a purpose. They aren't just random plays, fun tactics, or meaningless plans with no goal in sight. Of course not. They are all intended to be executed in order to win the game, the regionals, and ultimately the final championship. The goal is to be victorious and win! No argument there.

The spiritual battle you are in (and have been in) has an ultimate purpose as well. As discussed, you are in the middle of the fiercest war of all time. Fiercer than any game or tournament you have ever participated in, and it is the war between God and Satan.

They are in a fight for your SOUL and SPIRIT.

Please do not take that lightly and do not underestimate the nature of the battle because in the end you will either win or lose right along with the spiritual force you have aligned yourself with.

That is the ultimate race and you must find yourself on the right side at the end of it. This book is intended to help you get on the right path so that you can claim victory throughout the race as well as at the end. It all matters, and God has led you to this resource to help you understand this and to lean on Him to help you get there. He is the ONLY way you can win.

There is one final concept to break down.

This may be difficult to hear, but frankly we all have to hear it and face it because it applies to everyone.  We are all in the same race and we are all at the mercy of the enemy until we discover the truth of God.  At which point, we have the choice to believe God and allow Him access into our lives to help us overcome the enemy, or we can choose to reject God and continue on our own and follow the lies of our greatest opponent.

If we reject God while we are living and breathing, we will come to understand the truth after we pass.  Sadly, that is too late to make adjustments in our beliefs (repent).  We will then have to live in eternity with the spiritual forces that we listened to while on the earth.  That will not be pleasant and in fact, it will be far worse than you can imagine.  So please understand that this spiritual war, this unseen race that you are in right now, is one you have to get right. You do not have the strength, equipment, understanding, or weapons to successfully win on your own.

When you believe that Jesus died for you and paid your ultimate penalty, you are believing that He is the one who defeated your greatest enemy, because He is the only one who can.

Believing in Him is the start and it eternally secures you.

But why does the enemy persist you ask?  If I am eternally secure in Jesus, why would Satan continue to attack me?

That is a great question, and it relates DIRECTLY to your purpose.

Once you are sealed by God, Satan cannot remove that no matter what he tries.  God is clear about that and we have discovered that truth in earlier chapters. However, when God saves and seals you, He has put you in this battle as a warrior and He desires that you go to battle for Him.

His battle looks different than what you might naturally think or believe. Although you are familiar with football games, volleyball matches, track meets, or baseball games, and perhaps might have been looking for your purpose in these opportunities, they are only vehicles to be used by either God or the enemy.

Your purpose does not lie in your sport or in your athletic ability. Your purpose in the eyes of God, lies in Him.

The enemy has secretly attacked you for years, most likely through your athletic ability, success, and failures. It has been a secret attack because you were literally unaware that you had an enemy like this, and you were unaware that he was the source of the toxicity you were swimming in.

His goal was to keep you in a state of deception and blindness so that you would continue to fight against his forces in the natural. He knows this fight is spiritual, so he continued to come at you and watched you try to overcome his tactics in your own strength and awareness.

If he would have kept you blind and unaware of God, you would have continued on this path (in this race) and he would have claimed victory over your spirit when it was time for you to cross the finish line.

His strategy was to keep YOU blind and focused on reacting and responding to the multitude of voices shaping you, demanding performance, and expecting worldly outcomes and accomplishments from you. A life of struggle, pride, and agony. At the end of the day, what the enemy has done in this scenario, has been to cause you to exalt the praises and approval of others around you, and forced you to look at yourself as the only one who can please them.

This is a cycle of idolatry.

Please hear me out because I know that might be difficult to comprehend or swallow. But please remember that every single person on this planet has their own battle with idolatry, but the venue may be different for others. It may not be sports, but it may be their career, money, attention, lust, or any number of things that cause them to strive and perform absent of God.

In the end, if Satan can get everyone to believe that they are the answer to overcoming challenges in life, then he has been successful convincing them that they don't need God. They just need themselves. This may offer some temporary "wins" in life, but it does not and will not help in the ultimate spiritual battle for their spirit. That fight, that battle, that race is not of flesh and blood as you recall, and flesh and blood does not have eternal life. Only the spirit does.

Satan's primary strategy is to keep you (and others) blind to the truth that they need God. If he can do this successfully, then he has claimed that person.

But you have now received and believed in God's plan of redemption. You are eternally secure. Why won't the enemy leave you alone now?

He won't. That is correct.

Now that he can't claim your spirit, he will continue to feverishly attack you so that you do NOT fulfill the purpose that God has for you. This purpose is so valuable and is such a high calling, that the enemy will do all he can to sabotage it.

He knows that you now have the ultimate weapon against him, and now that he cannot claim you, he will shift his strategy to do all he can to prevent you from sharing God with others. He needs to keep as many people blinded to God as possible, so he will continue to attack you in an effort to keep you silent so that you do not activate your God-given purpose.

Now you see the beginnings of your purpose, and you can see that it perhaps has nothing to do with performance, personal accomplishments, or claiming a national title of some sort. Those are all temporal, earthly experiences that have caused a significant amount of stress and agony in your life. Those performance objectives have been driving you for years and have caused a great deal of suffering because of all the weeds that have been planted and grown to maturity throughout this process.

You have given 1000% of your existence to achieve, accomplish, and claim victory. And you have found your talents, abilities, and drive have all worked together to defeat you. All at your own personal expense.

That may sound discouraging, but let me remind you, being at the rock bottom of "you" is exactly where God wants you to be. When you have come to the end of yourself, you have reached a point of needing Him. That is precisely where you need to be so that He can take up the battle for you and you can rest and stop the futile performance that has led you here.

I do not know the specific purpose that God has for your life. Neither do you. However, He knows, and he will guide you into it now that He can. What I can assure you is that He will use your gifts and talents to fulfill your purpose, and He will equip you with the tools so that you can accomplish it. His purpose for you will not shine any lights on you.  They will shine the light on Him - *through you.*

What an amazing blessing and honor.  To be used for God and to have a very high spiritual calling upon your life.  He knows your drive, He knows your competitiveness, and He knows your boldness.  He will use those qualities to deliver and execute the purpose He has just for you.

Begin praying to ask Him to reveal what He wants for you to do. He will.  He will respond when you ask Him and He will answer your prayers.  You may not see the outcomes right away, but you will when the race has been finished.  He will reveal to you how your purpose helped others and advanced His Kingdom.

It will all be worth it, and there will be no greater reward when you cross the finish line and hear God speak these words to you:

*"His lord said to him, 'Well done, good and faithful servant; you have been faithful over a few things, I will make you ruler over many things. Enter into the joy of your lord" Matthew 25:23*

That is your ultimate victory.

# Chapter 14

# Coaches

The next couple of chapters will be for your coaches and parents, the most powerful influencers in your life as an athlete. The messages will be intended to help them - help you.

For the coaches.

First, let me be the one to say thank you.

Coaches are perhaps one of the greatest influences an athlete will ever have in their life. Many of you are involved in coaching because you love sport and because you value the opportunity to develop the athletic skills of the youth eagerly wanting to learn and improve.

You have a tremendous opportunity to powerfully affect and influence the life of countless young, impressionable kids and young adults. It is a significant responsibility and whether you may realize this or not, your influence will very likely remain with every athlete you encounter. Your coaching intersects with their developmental and formative years, so your footprint on their lives will be probably more powerful than anyone can really imagine.

I want to take this time to speak to coaches. This will not be intended to throw criticisms or condemnations your way. In fact, it will be the opposite, because of the incredibly persuasive role you have in the lives of many aspiring athletes.

It is not a big secret that sports and athletics have grown exponentially in the past 25-30 years. I think if we were all being honest, we could say that it has taken on a life of its own and has developed into a cultural beast. So much so, that it may appear to be daunting and formidable and that you, as the coach, are at its mercy. Especially those coaches who are involved with elementary school, middle school, and high school aged athletes.

I believe there is some truth to that notion, because if we unpack this beast, we will see the endless, repeat cycles of organized sports available through the school districts. Many athletes are multi-sport athletes and they participate in all the athletic opportunities available to them.

Then you examine the next layer of athletics available, which in all likelihood is more demanding and generates more pressures than organized sports through the education systems. The travelling, elite, specialized sports have been added to the already demanding life of the athlete attempting to stay on top of their academics, go to practice every day, and even try to work a side job here and there in the middle of it all to learn responsibility and earn a little money.

With the advent of the travelling teams, the athlete is now caught in the vortex of this momentum, and they believe that it is necessary for them to participate if they want to advance their athletic career, have a shot at becoming the best, and get recognized by scouts, recruiters, and universities.

This is not necessarily negative because if parents agree to pay for these opportunities, they are perhaps investing in their child's talents to aid them in securing a collegiate scholarship. At face value, that appears smart and wise. It perhaps is-especially if their child wants to participate. If the child wants to and doesn't feel compelled to because it is expected somehow, then maybe this is a good idea.

Perhaps what coaches should evaluate, when organizing and planning these travelling tournaments, events, and athletic opportunities, is that they are packing them onto the backs of young kids who are already locked into heavy obligations just by nature of being a student athlete. A reality that they cannot excuse themselves from. I don't know of any student who chooses not to participate in school athletics so that they can exclusively participate in the travelling opportunities. Maybe this does exist, however, it is likely rare.

As a coach for the school district, and as a coach for an elite travelling team, I implore you to give strong consideration to both athletic pathways, and maintain awareness that the athlete you are coaching is looking to you for decisions related to their athletic experiences.

Organized sports have many parameters, limitations, and restrictions built into their delivery and execution. Even athletics at the NCAA level has even greater parameters and restrictions designed to protect the athlete from excessive demands or overuse of their physical bodies. Perhaps there are other reasons behind these restrictions, but clearly there is a recognition that limits are needed and they may inherently assist in protecting the athlete from burn-out.

Limits and parameters are not the enemy. In today's world, they actually serve more as an ally or teammate than an opponent to overcome.

What can be done in this very real environment? With the organized sports, the plethora of travelling teams, and the overwhelming weight, pressure, and unsustainable life cycle of all these forces being carried on the shoulders of young kids, something has to give.

It is my belief that virtually everyone sees this, knows this, and worries about this truth. But the momentum is already drawing everyone into its funnel cloud and it will soon develop into a raging, relentless tornado and begin to destroy what is in its path.

That is a dramatic illustration, however, most of us are watching it happen right in front of us and aren't heeding the warnings.

Coaches, you have a lot of influence in this scenario. I am mostly speaking to the traveling team coaches, but am also including coaches involved in the school systems as well.

In the good ol' days, it was common practice to push the athletes to the point of exhaustion. It was viewed as weak for a coach to allow an athlete to take a break to get a drink. The mindset was to physically train the athlete so hard that they would learn internal strength, stamina, and be obedient to the instructions of their coach.

At face value, there isn't a lot wrong with that scenario, because strength does develop by being challenged and pushed beyond perceived limits. Stamina is developed by persistent training beyond the point of wanting to give up. And obedience is necessary to help train the athlete to respond to authority, especially in challenging situations.

Please know that these are all excellent teaching moments and they do build many important traits and characteristics in young athletes, even though they are difficult. Difficulty and challenge are not at question here. I want to convey that loud and clear. Often, today's culture caters too far the other way and does everything to help an individual avoid difficulties and challenges. This mindset is not good and all it does is limit the person and keeps them from recognizing their own abilities and strength (among other things).

What I am calling into question is the amount and level of difficulty and challenge we are heaping onto our children. That is the beast. It is not the athletic opportunity. It's the number of them.

As a coach, you can attempt to keep all this in mind and perhaps do your part not to push too hard or engage in too many opportunities. What I mean by that is that we have learned that getting a drink of water is not a sign of weakness. We have all evolved from that mindset and those days are now behind us when we thought we were doing the athlete a favor by heaping on repetitive drills and denying them a water break.

We know the error of our ways now as we have had to learn because of adverse situations that have forced rules to be changed in order to allow frequent water breaks.

We are seeing similar symptoms of "dehydration" in our athletes today. Not because they can't access water, but because they can't access oxygen.

The demands, the number of tournaments, the number of games, the time spent in buses and cars traveling to countless destinations, the number of wins and personal contributions, the number of weeknights, and the number of weekends that are expected are *beyond* out of control.

It's not just "getting crazy", it has surpassed crazy. And it is all on the shoulders of young, developing children who are not equipped to handle the level of weight, expectation, responsibility, or stresses on their minds, bodies, or spirits.

They cannot speak up and they will not speak up.

They will, however, act out and communicate through their behavior. Loud and clear.

What coaches envision for their athletes is to become the greatest version of themselves on and off the court, or on and off the field. That is the hope of all coaches because let's face it, if we can produce, train, and inspire our athletes to perform at their peak, we stand the best chance of winning the game or tournament. It makes sense and it is a noble pursuit.

But what is happening, is that the athlete who has tremendous potential, has carried an entire athletic career that should only span 10 years or so, on their backs as young children. So instead of producing this all-state athlete, which perhaps they have the potential to accomplish, many of these kids quit all sports before they even hit high school. If they don't quit by the time they reach high school, I can guarantee you that many of them WANT TO QUIT.

Talk about failing our children.

Talk about eliminating their God-given talents.

Talk about destroying their spirit before it can even take a breath.

The adults must listen to what our young athletes are NOT saying, but are communicating loud and clear. When they quit sports, they are saying "I hate this" "I don't want to continue like this", "I won't participate in this". They now have the voice of reason, and sadly, it is perhaps at their own athletic expense.

Coaches, you need to set limits on the number of games, tournaments, and practice demands. If you don't, you will be your team's own worst opponent because your pursuit to win on the backs of these young athletes, will leave you without a roster in which to accomplish your victories.

Limits and restrictions won't harm the athlete, they will allow them to have sufficient internal resources to contribute. When athletes have internal resources, they will be able to contribute to the success of the team. Remember it is not just what you are demanding of them, your expectations are heaped on top of all the other athletic and academic demands that extend well beyond your view and reach.

Just because your roster has to be locked in a year in advance, doesn't mean you have to schedule tournaments on every weekend, through the off-season, or every weekend during the season. Please stop doing that. It is not required, and it is not a good idea. Stack more during the season but keep them to zero or just a few during the remainder of the year. That goes against conventional wisdom, but clearly conventional wisdom is not very wise.

Heed the warnings and take shelter from the ominous funnel clouds that you can clearly see. You don't have to allow your athletes and your team to get swept up in the vortex of an F-5 tornado that will destroy all that is in its path.

# Chapter 15

# Parents

Parents are the ultimate advocates for their child.  They are the ultimate voice for their child, and so it should be.  Kids aren't mature enough or developed to make appropriate decisions for themselves.  We all understand that and grasp the concept.

But as a parent, it can be difficult to know the best way to advocate for your child, especially when they are athletically gifted.  Any parent wants to provide as many opportunities as possible for their athletic child so they can develop their God-given talents, contribute to a winning team, and propel their athletic careers to the next level.

That is fabulous parenting in anyone's book.  I could break that down in a million ways and illustrate the powerful and positive influence this has on your child.  It is not a negative and it is not a poor reflection of your parenting.

Most of us want what is best for our children and we do all we can, sacrifice what we can, and pursue as many opportunities as possible to maximize the potential in our kids.  That is perhaps the greatest gift we can offer them, in all aspects of life, including athletics.

But, like almost every parent likely wonders, when is enough, enough? How can I stop this powerful momentum that has already been set in motion without compromising my child's athletic abilities or career?

It is enormously difficult. Setting limits and boundaries may likely cause heavy backlash, criticism, and harsh rebukes from coaches, other parents, and even our own children. Not a popular seat to be sitting in, especially if your child is athletically talented and wants to pursue the opportunities available.

It is easy to see how almost all parents are almost forced into this culture and feel as though they too, are at its mercy.

Perhaps, in some ways this is a real phenomenon, and there really are no good answers. However, we cannot lose sight of the fact that our job as a parent is to balance the advocacy efforts for our children. What I mean is that we can advocate for athletic opportunities, however, we must continue to advocate for their delicate bodies, spirit, and minds. If we understand that we have to be their voice by setting limits and boundaries in other areas of their lives, because they aren't mature enough to do this on their own, then we have to apply that to athletics as well.

They will possibly demand to participate in three travelling teams, organized sports through school, and recreation ball as a nine-, ten-, or eleven-year-old. But what the pre-adolescent cannot possibly understand is that they are demanding to be overwhelmed, burnt out, and angry by the time they are 15 years old. They are demanding to learn to hate sports, practices, games, tournaments, and meets. They are demanding to force themselves to quit or desperately want to quit by the time they reach high school. They are demanding to end their athletic career prematurely and never realize their true potential.

They are relying on their parents to make difficult decisions for them, and to set limits and boundaries for them because they do not know what is in their best interest, and they cannot stand up (and should not be expected to) against the depth of the forces they do not understand.

Where does a parent even start? The whipping, circling, and spinning winds are drawing you all into its vortex as well. The twisting nature of this momentum is very difficult to resist. If not careful, it will hold you captive in its powerful energy and when it releases you, the landscape will look dramatically different, and you might have to begin to rebuild and reconstruct. That is often difficult to do after significant devastation.

Please prioritize the mental, spiritual, and physical needs of your child over the athletic. Begin to see the athletic opportunities as an avenue for your child to grow, develop, and refine their mental, spiritual, and physical abilities. The competitive nature of sports is a wonderful opportunity to help your child enhance their lives, build their internal strength, and learn to respond to a team and a coach who all work together to accomplish a common goal.

That is an amazing opportunity and gift that you can provide your athletic child.

Setting limits will allow your child to continue to develop. It will not stunt their abilities, eliminate opportunities, or forfeit their future. It will likely do the opposite, because it will not unwittingly drill their talents into the ground before they actually reach an age to be noticed by a scout, recruiter, or University athletics.

Seek a traveling team that limits the number of games and tournaments-especially in the off seasons. Consider allowing only one sport through a traveling organization for your child to participate in.  Even if they have multi-sport athletic talent.  Allow them to choose just one elite organization to participate in.

Most college coaches value multi-sport athletes, and they can recognize the pure authentic ability that a multi-sport athlete possesses.  These coaches seek out pure athleticism because they know that the technical skills and raw talent are there.  They just need to offer scholarship aid and find a place on the team to tap into that natural talent.  These coaches don't look at how many games and tournaments the athlete has played in, they evaluate natural talent and athletic skill.

If the athlete is so burned out, angry, and hates sports before they finish middle school, this talent will never be discovered, and the ultimate opportunity will never be there.  And if it is, today's athletic culture will run the risk of sending a talented athlete to college and they are smoldering in fear, anxiety, exhaustion, and internal defeat.

If you have more than one athletic child, how on earth....................

Heed the warnings.  You see them, hear them, and feel them.

# Chapter 16

# Water Break

The next few chapters will be targeting specific struggles that you likely experience as an athlete. They are going to be focused on helping you exercise spiritual strategies to combat the forces coming against you. As discussed, you will continue to receive attacks from the enemy, so allow these next few pages to help you when you begin to feel the toxins from the poisonous weeds that may still need rooted out or have been allowed to sneak in and take root.

As the opening line of this book states, "This book is written especially for you."

It is intended to help you in all ways, so please reference the next few chapters when you begin feeling familiar stressors that manifest in the form of anxiety, depression, and the like. The content will be arranged more like a devotional to help you target specific feelings, and to properly address them so that God can help you claim victory over those battles along the way.

**Disclaimer: These devotional areas are not intended to replace the support and guidance of a qualified professional Christian Counselor. I encourage you to seek these resources should you need mental health support. The following**

chapters are intended to guide you in prayer, offer possible insights into why you might be experiencing toxic feelings, and scripture to back it up.

# Chapter 17

# Depression

## Prayer

Lord,

My heart is heavy and trodden down with the weight of depression. I am feeling the dense fog surround my thoughts and begin to infiltrate my life. I am reaching out to you to help me lift this heaviness, to help me clear the density of these feelings, and to heal the brokenness I feel inside me. You have given me so much opportunity and so much to be thankful for, and I want to experience the joy that you have for me.

I know that you have given me plenty, and with that comes great responsibility. I welcome that, but the burden feels heavy at times, and I feel I am sinking and drowning in everything going on in my life. I am boldly coming to you to help me, to heal me, to lift me out of these dark waters and to put me on the path of joy and healing that you have for me.

As I reach to you for healing, and surrender the sense of depression I am in, I am asking that you help shift my eyes onto others who are suffering as well. Allow me to recognize them and to reach out in ways that you know they need.  I pray that you put people who need you in my path so that I can possibly touch their lives and offer just a little of what they might need so they find you.

I am praying that you help me to forgive anyone who has hurt me, harmed me, abused me, or caused any pain in my life that may be contributing to this sense of depression.  I know that I cannot forgive some people on my own, so I am asking for your help to release the pain they have caused in my heart.  I will pray for you to help me release and forgive them as many times as it is necessary, so that I can be free of that wound contributing to the lack of joy I am experiencing right now.

I know you desire for me to have joy.  I am seeking you right now to help me regain that joy in my heart.

Amen.

# Insights

Many of us deal with some level of depression at some point in our lives.  Some of us carry it with us for years.  It is a dark heaviness that truly does steal our joy and seems to consume our heart and emit its own energy through us.

Life is hard and perhaps it has introduced you to some experiences that have deeply hurt you.  Maybe you have been the victim of willful abuse and neglect of someone that was supposed to care about you.  Maybe you have been the victim of complying with the demands of another when you really didn't want to.  Or perhaps people in your life have hurt you because of their actions and decisions, and caused wounds, even if they didn't intend to hurt you.

There are countless reasons we experience trauma, and often when we do, there are a myriad of feelings attached to the experience. If the wounding is so profound perhaps there is deep seated anger that has never been recognized or expressed, but instead just buried and hidden because to express it causes you to fear their rejection.

Examine your life. Examine the experiences and people who have hurt you either willfully, or by extension of their decisions. Examine your athletic career and consider the moments, situations, and voices who have haunted you, caused you fear, or created doubt and distress.

With each of these injuries comes pain and even anguish in some cases. Perhaps this pain has not been resolved because it has been intentionally buried and shoved aside so that you can continue to function and perform as you needed to. For their approval, and for your athletic survival.

If this is true, perhaps there is unresolved pain and anger.

*What if depression was really pain and anger turned inward?*

If you think about it, it makes a lot of sense. I think the Bible addresses this as well when it encourages and strongly advises us to forgive each other.

Forgiveness does not equate to condoning behavior that has been harmful. It does not mean that you should resume a relationship with someone who has abused you. It does not suggest that you jump right back into an unhealthy situation. Those are the assumptions we make.

What if unforgiveness really means pain and anger? What if it is God's way of identifying all the wounds, pain, anger, emotional injuries we have is to package them all up and label them as unforgiveness?

If we can release this unforgiveness, then we can extract its poison and perhaps begin to eliminate the depression that consumes our hearts and lives. It might sound counterintuitive; however, it is worth every bit of mental imagery and prayer to ask God to take it out of your heart. It is worth every prayer where you visualize the person who has hurt you and ask God to remove the unforgiveness that you have for them, even if you can't feel it or recognize it. Do this over and over. He will help you because He has commanded you to forgive. Even your enemies.

Perhaps this command is not simply to force you into compliance. Perhaps is a command to free your heart of the things that could be causing or contributing to your depression. God will help you. He is bigger than this, and He has equipped you with the command to forgive so that you can find the joy He has promised you.

*"And be kind to one another, tenderhearted, forgiving one another, even as God in Christ forgave you" Ephesians 4:32*

*"Fear not, for I am with you; be not dismayed, for I am your God; I will strengthen you, I will help you, I will uphold you with my righteous right hand" Isaiah 41:10*

*"Come to me, all who are heavy laden, and I will give you rest" Matthew 11:28*

# Chapter 18

# Anxiety

## Prayer

Lord,

I feel the never-ending electrical current coursing through both my body and heart.  It feels like it is just beneath my skin, and I cannot find peace.  These jolts of unease are relentless, and they stab at my skin like they are trying to rip it open to be released.  I feel like I am held hostage inside my body and entrapped within this internal, electrical fence relentlessly sending waves of electricity through me.

I know that I have placed immense pressure upon myself to perform and even to find perfection at times.  I know that in my efforts to do that, I have developed a deep sense of fear that I will disappoint people who are important to me, and I fear that I will not do well in my sport.  If I were to be honest, I feel almost unworthy at times to be here because it seems like I am living someone else's life.  I have lost my identity and turned into an image that has been created by others.  I know that wasn't their intent.  I know that wasn't my intent.  But here I am.  Trying to achieve the expectations of this image. That is impossible, but I am still trying.

My quest for perfection and for accomplishing the demands of this image has created fear deep inside me. Fear of failure, fear of rejection, fear of under-performing, and fear of defeat. I know this fear has begun to surface in me and is causing the tightness in my muscles, the panic in my heart, and the jagged current coursing through my veins.

I am reaching to you Lord, to help me focus on you and not the voices of others. Help me hear your voice of encouragement and contentment, so that I can begin to allow your voice to lead and guide me. Not the others who are perhaps contributing to my fear of failure and disapproval.

I know you want me to be at peace. That is your desire for me. I am reaching to you to help me find that peace and to take authority over the fear that has no place in my heart or my life. I will call upon your name to cancel any spirit of fear that tries to make its way into my mind. I will take your authority and demand that the spirit of fear, the spirit of pleasing others, the spirit of perfection leave my mind and leave my heart. Your word tells me that those are of the enemy and that I have your authority to command them to leave.

I cancel and rebuke any and all spirits of fear from my life in the name and authority of Jesus Christ. You have to flee, and I command that you permanently chain yourselves to the gates of hell.

I pray this in the authority of Jesus Christ,

Amen.

# Insights

The bible says that you should not live in fear. It also says that believers do not have a spirit of fear. However, you feel consumed by it and its ravaging side effects of anxiety and worry. Anyone who has experienced never-ending anxiety often knows that they are suffering, but don't really consider that they don't have to live that way.

Has anxiety become so engrained in your life that you just believe it is a part of your personality, who you are, and such a normal experience that you haven't even considered that it's *abnormal*? Or have you considered that you are harboring deep fears that might contribute to the cause of these toxic sensations?

Fear can be deeply rooted in our hearts, and it has tremendous influence over our perceptions and behaviors. When fear has reached the point of terribly uncomfortable anxiety, we do things to numb the sensations, seek ways to find comfort, and even make attempts to run away from it.

Typically, these reactions are loudly communicating that we are being passive and carry a victim mentality when it comes to addressing these fears. Fear is of the enemy, and the enemy does NOT HAVE POWER. If we ignore fear, try to numb it, or run away from it, WE are giving it power to wreak havoc in our lives.

God tells us we do not have the spirit of fear as a believer, but that doesn't mean it is an automatic transformation. It means that we have HIS power and authority and should access it immediately to get it out of our lives. Remember, God has the power, but He will patiently wait for you to access it and use it. He is not controlling.

He is equipping, which means His authority is available to you to use as you need to.

When you execute His authority, you are no longer a victim. You are taking charge of your life, and you can command your fears to leave. If you take authority over fear, by using the authority of Jesus to remove any and all spirits of fear, you will realize God's promise that as a believer, you do NOT have a spirit of fear.

Fear is your greatest enemy.

God is your greatest weapon, and His authority will eliminate any fear that you have been living in.

Exercise HIS authority and take control of your mind, heart, and body.

*"For God has not given us a spirit of fear, but of power and of love and of a sound mind" 2 Timothy 1:7*

*"There is no fear in love; but perfect love casts out fear, because fear involves torment. But he who fears has not been made perfect in love" John 4:18 NKJV*

*"Be anxious for nothing, but in everything by prayer and supplication, with thanksgiving, let your requests be made known to God" Philippians 4:6*

# Chapter 19

# Self-Indulgence Sin

## *Prayer*

Lord,

With so many external and internal pressures, I feel the weight of it all on my shoulders. I find myself wanting to get away from it all and when I do, I find myself engaging in behaviors that I know are not pleasing to you. I find myself seeking moments of pleasure and escape, just so I can numb my feelings or counter them with indulgent sins of my flesh.

I know what is sinful and I know that my behavior is not always pleasing to you. It affects me as well, and I am seeking your forgiveness. I am seeking your help in giving me the strength to overcome these temptations and to shape my heart in a way that pursues you more than the temptation.

I know that I will always be imperfect because I live in the flesh, which is constantly self-serving, and seeking gratification. I am asking you to mature my spirit so that I can become more victorious over these moments and that you can see my heart is desiring more and more to please you.

I am so thankful that you sent your son Jesus Christ to die, be buried, and resurrected to pay the penalty for all my sins, including these. I am not able to save myself, and I humbly believe that Jesus can save me, and has saved me.

Help me to develop the self-control that is promised through You. Help me to continue to seek your Word and its truth that will help me grow into the purpose that you have for me, so that I can glorify You in the process.

I humbly ask for you to strengthen me against my enemies, and that You create a heart in me that is in search of You.

Amen.

# Insights

Self-indulgence and sin.

It is pretty difficult to hide and it tee's up the critics for secret and open mocking and scoffing. When you have a sensitivity towards what others say and think about you, this can be a bit much to cope with.

But rest assured, although God hates sin, it must be repeated, that He LOVES you. He is well aware that we all live in flesh. We have covered the fact that the flesh is constantly striving for gratification, and we are simply wired that way. We will seek gratification at some level, and we will cave to the demands of the flesh.

God does not expect us to be perfect. In fact, he states in the Bible that anyone who claims that they are without sin is a liar. That has to be true because if it were not true, why would he have sent His own PERFECT (sinless) son to die a brutal death for the sins of the entire world?  If we could be sinless and perfect in the flesh without Jesus, He would have made that clear and He would not have sent Jesus to die on the cross for our sins.  It would not have been necessary.

So, rest easy.  Your sin is no worse than the mockers and scoffers who might be calling you a hypocrite to your face, on social media, or behind your back in a circle of your friends.

The difference is that you have the remedy for your sin, they do not.  You have propitiation for your sin.  They likely do not.  You have had your sins washed away and removed as far as the east is to the west.  They likely have not.

Give your transgressions to God, surrender them to Him.  He says to cast your cares upon Him and that includes your self-indulgence, your behaviors that are not pleasing to Him, and your imperfections.  Do not allow your perfection-seeking nature try to convince you that you cannot be forgiven.

Do not allow the "religious" critics to convince you that if you sin, you will lose your salvation.  If you are saved, you are saved. Jesus is the ONLY way to salvation.

If Jesus is the ONLY way to salvation, then how can anyone, as a human living in a sinful body, have any power to sustain their own salvation? They can't.  No matter how religious they are, no matter how perfect they think they are, and no matter how much someone has convinced themselves that they don't sin.  These people believe that they can sustain their own salvation through their own behavior.

I would caution against this mindset.

Why?

Well, it seems that most can agree that Jesus Christ is the only way to salvation, and that we can't do one thing to perform through our actions and behaviors to save ourselves.  We all need Jesus to save us.

However, if we think we have all of a sudden developed supernatural power after we are saved, and somehow, we can then SUSTAIN our salvation, then are we in a round about way dismissing Jesus?  Are we saying to Jesus, "Hey thanks for the lead in, but I got this now.  I don't need you.  My behavior and my works will take it from here to make sure I get into heaven."

Perhaps that is not a literal conversation, however, it is unarguably the message they are sending and the mindset that they have.  A very dangerous position to be in, and a very slippery slope when it comes to understanding the gospel.

So, instead of allowing critics to beat us up over our behavior, our sin, and our indulgences, why don't we take those things to God, ask for help and forgiveness, and pray for them.

*That* is the demonstration of the maturity of Christ. Not self-appointed perfection.

Our salvation is through belief in Jesus Christ alone.  Not our performance, or our works. *Jesus did the work.*  We have to have faith and believe it.

*"If we say that we have no sin, we deceive ourselves, and the truth is not in us" 1 John 1:8*

*"For God so loved the world that He gave His only So, that whoever believes in Him should not perish but have eternal life" John 3:16*

*"Whoever believes in the Son has eternal life, but whoever rejects the Son will not see life, for God's wrath remains on them" John 3:36*

*"For my Father's will is that everyone who looks to the Son and believe in Him shall have eternal life, and I will raise them up at the last day" John 6:40*

# Chapter 20

# Performance

Because this book is intended to reach you as an athlete, it can clearly be meaningful for everyone. Although the pressures and life situations might look different for others, the same landscape, seeds, ground, soil, and plant analogy applies.

But for you in particular, performance has been a major driving force in your life, and it can continue to get tangled up in your faith as well. It has likely become so intertwined in your life as an athlete, that it will perhaps be a challenge for you to disassemble this thought process and subsequent behaviors as it relates to your spiritual walk.

Grasping this may take time and spiritual maturity. It does for many people. However, most of us simply want to apply performance to salvation because it is natural, and it is what we know.

But God's word is clear. You cannot ever behave good enough, do enough good deeds, or perform at high enough levels to earn your way into heaven. You cannot earn redemption.

Many don't realize this at all, and you can see them doing all kinds of things that make them appear to be good people. Good enough to earn a spot in the heavenly realm after they pass on. Perhaps they will be in heaven, however, the scriptures are very clear that it is not related to their good deeds, their "good outweighing their bad" or their efforts to be in church every time the doors open.

In no way am I trying to be critical of any good deeds, going to church, or serving others. I am not. What I am saying is that this is not what allows you entry into heaven. If you are saved and are doing these things to advance the Kingdom of God, then you are beautifully engaged in fulfilling the purpose that God has for you.

This is precisely where performance can and does deceive people.

If we do not know God's plan for salvation, we will naturally take on the performance plan and be convinced that our actions will be sufficient to get us into right standing with God. It is a very natural way of thinking, and it is a very natural way of acting. We do this all the time for our sport, our career, and our earthly pursuits. Why wouldn't that apply to our spiritual lives as well?

Remember that God does not operate in the flesh.

He actually has provided an entire book in the form of the Holy Bible to SAVE US from the flesh.

If we are not saved from our flesh (aka sin), then we will be eternally separated from Him. Many people don't even know this. They have been deceived into believing their performance as a "good person" will be sufficient to keep them on the path leading of them to the Lord.

Unless they discover that they are in complete error, they will unwittingly continue down the same path, look great in the eyes of their peers, but hear God say to them, "depart from me, I never knew you" on their day of judgement.

Performance is found nowhere in the message of the gospel.

That should help you breathe a little easier because, well are you sick of performing? Wouldn't it be scary to think that you had to perform to get into heaven? How much is enough? What is good enough? Where is the bar? What is considered a victory?

Talk about stress.

The gospel, the salvation message, the path to heaven, and the requirements for redemption all lie in a person's faith and belief in the GIFT of Jesus Christ.

Faith and belief are in direct opposition to performance.

That should not be too surprising after learning that God's spiritual promises, truths, and messages are all in opposition to the natural. They are opposing forces, and the flesh produces nothing but sin. Good works of the flesh without God can be helpful for someone, but it accounts for nothing in your spiritual journey. In fact, it will just be burnt up as if it were wood, hay, or stubble.

It served its momentary purpose, and it will have no life beyond that moment.

So, as we are wrapping this up, it is important to reflect back one more time on the wheat and weed analogy. There are many weeds that you can remove and eliminate in your life, and we discussed those throughout the chapters of this book. But there is one weed that resembles the stalk of wheat. it is referred to as a tare. If you know anything about agriculture, you have probably heard of a tare. But if you are like most of us, you have no idea what it is.

However, God tells us that the wheat and the tares grow together. They do resemble each other, so it is impossible for the harvester to discern which is the authentic plant and which is the weed. In the end, when the crop has matured, the wheat and the tare will be harvested together. They will then go through a violent threshing process to separate them. When this threshing process is complete, the authentic wheat will be gathered and its look alike tare will be separated, burned and destroyed.

This threshing process is extremely difficult and tumultuous, but you can see how necessary it is to allow for the final harvesting process to be completed.

As in your life, and many others, you have had to go through violent, challenging experiences to break your will to the point of allowing seeds to be planted, take root, and grow. When it is time for God to harvest His own, He will have to determine if His roots are within you. When this final harvest takes place, God will separate the wheat from the tares, and you will want to make sure that you are with the authentic wheat, and not the look alike.

*"The kingdom of heaven is like a man who sowed good seed in his field; but while men slept, his enemy came and sowed tares among the wheat and went his way. But when the grain had sprouted and produced a crop, then the tares also appeared. So, the servants of the owner came and said to him, 'Sir, did you not sow good seed in your field? How then does it have tares?' He said to them, 'An enemy has done this.' The servants said to him, 'Do you want us then to go and gather them up?' But he said, 'No, lest while you gather up the tares you also uproot the wheat with them. Let both grow together until the harvest, and at the time of harvest I will say to the reapers, "First gather together the tares and bind them in bundles to burn them, but gather the wheat into my barn" Matthew 13:24-30*

There is only one way. It is a gift. Jesus Christ.

*"For the wages of sin is death, but the gift of God is eternal life in Christ Jesus our Lord" Romans 6:23*

*"For God did not send His Son into the world to condemn the world, but that the world through Him might be saved" John 3:17*

*"For by grace, you have been saved through faith, and that not of yourselves; it is the gift of God, not of works lest any many should boast" Ephesians 2:8*

So, continue to be the athlete that God created you to be.  Lean on Him to defeat your greatest opponent so that you can enjoy your athletics, contribute all that you can, and give Him the glory for your accomplishments.  He will reveal the important purpose He has for you, and He will work through you to fulfill it.

Above all, know this.  You are a child of the Most High God.

THAT is the real victory.

# REFERENCES:

Biblehub.com